# A BIRDWATCHERS' GUIDE TO PORTUGAL AND MADEIRA

## C. C. Moore, Gonçalo Elias and Helder Costa

Illustrations by Tony Disley

BIRD WATCHERS' GUIDES

Prion Ltd.
Perry

# ABOUT THE BOOK...

This book describes in detail 18 major sites in Mainland Portugal, as well as a further 14 minor sites like the Minho Estuary in the north-west and the Berlenga Archipelago, famed for its seabirds. A selection of the most interesting species found in the eighteen major sites has been tabulated at the end to facilitate easy referencing.

A section on seabirds, new to these guides, is also included, since Portuguese waters are rich in pelagic species such as Wilson's Petrel, as well as seabirds breeding in Macaronesian waters.

For ease of access, Madeira is dealt with separately in the second half of the book, especially as many birdwatchers fly directly to Madeira without ever visiting Continental Portugal.

Birdwatchers often come to southern Europe in search of specific species – Great Spotted Cuckoo and Red-necked Nightjar spring to mind. Thus selected lists of the most sought-after species to be found in Portugal and in Madeira are included in the relevant sections and finally complete annotated lists of all the birds seen in Portugal and Madeira are included at the end of the guide.

The maps of the larger areas in this guide only show main roads and tracks and one should buy some of the large scale maps as described in the Maps section.

# ACKNOWLEDGEMENTS

A very special thanks goes to Miguel Lecoq for his work on the Ria Formosa; Luís Gordinho put at our disposal a synthesis of his research on the Ria de Aveiro. These data, so freely given, made it possible to write comprehensive accounts of these two major Portuguese wetlands. Luís Gordinho also made a full revision of the first draft of this book.

Luís Reino and Pedro Geraldes provided information on sites in northern Portugal. Anabela Trindade and Paula Rito de Araújo provided mammal and reptile/amphibian lists, respectively.

Finally, we would like to thank our families for their forbearance during the gestation and birth of this book.

*C. C. Moore* is head of science in St Dominics, one of Lisbon's international schools and has lived a quarter of his life in Portugal. He is a founder member of the Portuguese Rarities Committee and has published over fifty papers on a variety of subjects from lichen ecology to bird topography.

*Gonçalo Lobo Elias*, though an engineer working on mobile communications, has devoted many years to birding activities. He has been an active ringer since 1992, is presently editing a book on winter atlas work and has published several papers on rare breeding birds in Portugal.

*Helder Costa*, when not engrossed in the banking business, is secretary of the Portuguese Rarities Committee, vice-president of SPEA (Portuguese Society for the Study of Birds) and has published a number of important papers on birds.

# CONTENTS

# INTRODUCTION

Portugal is a challenge for birdwatchers. It has the temperate forests of western Europe and the continental plains of the east; it is washed by a cold enriching current yet is climatically dominated by a subtropical anticyclone. Add to this its Vinho Verde (Green Wine) and its distinctive people and you have a country that is truly fascinating.

This small sliver of land in the south-west corner of Europe has had its moments. Home to a highly original culture in the fourth and third millennia B.C., wintering quarters to Carthaginian armies and a sphere of Roman influence by 60 B.C., Portugal saw Judeo-Christian and Islamic fervour and gained immeasurably by the cultural aftershock. Though the Portuguese Inquisition was terminated only in 1820, the two great dynasties that ruled Portugal from early in the 12th century to 1580 recognised Moorish and Jewish genius and thereby fulfilled Portugal's dream by discovering the world, often using regal prerogative to side-step church intolerance.

Colonial Portugal was immense and might have gone the way of peaceful transition after World War II. However, Oliveira Salazar propelled Portugal into colonial war, defeat and moral bankruptcy. Yet that subtle mix of peoples, the Portuguese, slow to burn, pragmatic and contradictory, brought about a bloodless revolution in 1974 at home and disengagement abroad.

Since then, Portugal has become an active member of Europe's latest alliance, the European Union, and has used its colonial experience to forge new links with Portuguese-speaking Africa and South America.

## Erratum
The tables on pages 117 and 120 have been transposed and appear out of order. The information contained in them is correct.

# PRE-TOUR INFORMATION

Travelling to Portugal is relatively document free. European Union nationals are allowed to enter the country bearing just a national identity card; people from other countries require a passport and, in many cases, a visa. Visitors are usually allowed a three-month stay, although citizens of a few countries have more limited visiting privileges. Citizens of non-European Union countries should check with the nearest Portuguese embassy or with a local travel agency for their entry requirements.

If travelling by car, you need a valid driving licence and car ownership papers. It is advisable to inform your car insurance company of your visit, as they can arrange suitable cover if you wish insurance over and above the basic 'green card'. You may not be asked to stop at the border when entering from Spain, as customs posts have been withdrawn, according to the rules of the European Union, where people and goods are subject to free circulation.

There are embassies or consulates of most countries in Lisbon. Furthermore, in Oporto there are consulates for 37 different countries. In Faro (Algarve) there are consular offices of Angola, Canada, Germany, Holland, and Norway, and in Portimão (Algarve) there are consular offices of the United Kingdom and Sweden. The addresses of all these offices are available in telephone books (in Portuguese, embassy is 'Embaixada', and consular office is 'Consulado').

The Portuguese currency is the Escudo (Esc.), and in November 1997 there were 290 escudos to the British pound. Although escudos can be purchased in most countries before travelling, it is preferable to obtain them upon arrival, as the exchange rate tends to be more favourable. The bank network is extensive and banks and cashpoint facilities exist in most towns and villages. Banks are open on weekdays, from 08.30 to 15.00 hrs and will readily accept most west European currencies or US Dollars. Exchange facilities also exist at the airports and are open until late in the day. Many stores, hotels, pensions and restaurants accept VISA and most other common credit cards, as well as Eurocheques, though these may prove less useful in remote inland areas and it is therefore recommended that you take some paper money with you.

Although it is easy to obtain print and transparency film in Portugal, prices tend to be higher than elsewhere in Europe and slide film may be non-existent in small towns or away from the coast. If you have a special brand preference or require specialised films, it is better to purchase them before you leave home.

No special vaccinations certificates are required from E.U. citizens wishing to enter Portugal. Citizens of some non-E.U. countries do have to show certificates of inoculation against certain diseases. If you think this might apply to you please contact your nearest Portuguese embassy or your travel agent for advice.

# TRAVEL INFORMATION

## Travelling to Portugal

There are three ways of getting to Portugal: by air, by rail or by road.
No car ferry or passenger lines regularly visit Portugal, but the car ferry
from Plymouth to Santander in Spain brings car owners within a day's
drive of Portugal.

By air, there are regular flights from most of the larger European
cities to Lisbon, Oporto and Faro. There are also many cheap charter
flights from European capitals to Portugal and your local travel agency
can often arrange flight and car hire simultaneously. All the above
mentioned airports are a bus ride away from their corresponding city
centres; taxis are still relatively inexpensive (ask for price in advance).

By rail, there are daily trains from Madrid to Lisbon and from Paris
to Lisbon and Oporto. This is certainly the least expensive option and
the most convenient one for those with limited pockets. The Inter-Rail
ticket and other special rail offers allow unlimited travel within Europe,
including Portugal. It should be emphasised, however, that the rail
network in Portugal is not very extensive and that for most
birdwatching sites rail travel is not a viable option.

Entering Portugal by car normally involves crossing Spain on the E3,
which leads from the French border through Valladolid and Salamanca
(Spain) and enters Portugal at Vilar Formoso. Other alternatives also
exist. The E4, which runs further south, from Madrid through Cáceres,
crosses the border at Caia, near Elvas. The E1/N431, which comes from
Seville, crosses the frontier over the recently built bridge at Castro
Marim, in the south-eastern corner of Portugal. These roads are of
international standard, but in summer or during holiday periods may
be overcrowded.

## Travelling within Portugal

By car is certainly the most convenient way to travel in Portugal; the
road network is quite extensive and provides access to most areas,
though it may be necessary to use rough tracks to approach the more
remote and interesting sites. A good map (see next section) will allow
you to travel through most of the country, with minimal navigation
skills required.

It is important to bear in mind that many metalled roads are in bad
condition and may be difficult to travel on. The A.C.P. map (see next
section) contains valuable information about road condition all over the
country.

In Portugal, the following categories of roads exist:

- Auto-estradas (Motorways), usually known as A1, A2, etc. These
  roads are not numerous, though the network is being expanded.
  The existing ones provide easy and speedy access to and from
  Lisbon and Oporto. The A1 connects Lisbon to Oporto, from where
  the A3 and A4 run northwards and eastwards, respectively.
  Around Lisbon, the A5 provides fast access to the western suburbs,
  while the A2 crosses the river and proceeds south-eastwards. The
  A6 leads eastwards through the Alentejo. A toll must be paid when
  using motorways (about 10 Esc./km in 1997).

- Main Roads (on sign posts marked IP=Itinerário Principal). These are modern toll-free roads, allowing rapid travel between the main cities. The IP1 runs from Oporto to Lisbon (via the A1) and then southwards to the Algarve (it is currently one of the most dangerous roads in the country). The IP2 runs from near Bragança in the north-east to Ourique near Beja in the south, where it joins the IP1. It is an inland route passing Guarda, Castelo Branco, Portalegre and Évora; however, only parts of it have been built. The IP3 runs from Coimbra to Viseu and provides a convenient way to travel from Lisbon to north-eastern Portugal, leaving the A1 at Coimbra, though it is not very safe in some parts. The IP4 runs from Oporto to Bragança. The IP5 leads from Aveiro through Viseu to Guarda and Vilar Formoso and is the main international road out of Portugal, and from Lisbon to the north-east, via Coimbra and the IP3. Finally, the IP6 runs from Torres Novas eastwards towards Castelo Branco.
- National Roads (N1, N123, N375, etc.), which form a dense network all over the country.
- Municipal Roads, of variable quality.

Cars can be rented for short or long periods and can often be arranged through a local travel agency before you leave home. As elsewhere this can be an expensive option and it may be cheaper to rent locally.

For those bringing right-hand drive cars to Portugal it is advisable to cover the prism of the headlights with a triangle of dark adhesive tape. Never stop on the left side of the road as the natural tendency is to set off again on that side. This can lead to situations ranging from the comic to the tragic. Cars on roundabouts have right of way unless clearly stated otherwise.

It is worth pointing out that road deaths are alarmingly high in Portugal and great care should be taken using roundabouts or minor roads or when parking to watch interesting species. The maximum speed limits for passenger cars are as follows: 120km/hr on motorways and on certain main roads, 90km/hr on all other roads and 50km/hr in urban zones (including small villages).

For local movement within cities, taxis are a useful form of transport. Within the larger cities, they are equipped with digital taximeters, but in small towns and outside urban areas it may be necessary to negotiate the price of the journey before you set off.

*Train*    Travelling by rail can be an interesting option and tickets are cheap, compared with most west European countries (Lisbon to Faro costs 3010 Esc. 1st class and 2060 Esc. 2nd class in 1997). For those not bringing their own car to Portugal, it is worth considering travelling by train and then renting a car in the area to be explored, as petrol and motorway tolls can prove very expensive. The rail network is not extensive; the only important tracks run from Lisbon to Oporto and from Lisbon to the Algarve, and these are of little use to the birdwatcher. Nevertheless, some sites can be reached by train, particularly the Boquilobo Marsh (served by local trains on the Lisbon-

Oporto line), as well as Faro, Ria de Alvor and Castro Marim (on the Algarve coastal line). All these sites can easily be explored on foot from the railway station. Other towns, such as Elvas and Castelo Branco (near International Tagus) can also be reached by train, but the enormous sites nearby are very difficult to explore effectively on foot. A train timetable is available in any of the main railway stations for 350 Esc. (1997 prices); it gives all the information necessary to travel by train in Portugal. The times can and should be checked against the latest wall timetables at the station well before departure.

*Buses*   Buses can also be used to reach several interesting areas, although, after arrival, extensive walking may be required to reach the more remote sites. Some important bus companies in Lisbon are listed below:

RODOVIÁRIA has a good express bus network to many towns and villages, including inland ones. General information and tickets can be obtained at the bus terminal, Avenida Casal Ribeiro, near Praça Duque de Saldanha (information is also available on the Internet at www.rede-expressos.pt).

RENEX , RESENDE and CAIMA run hourly buses from Lisbon to the Algarve, including Lagos, Portimão, Faro and Vila Real de Santo António, near Castro Marim. The bus terminal is at Campo das Cebolas, near Praça do Comércio and tickets cost 2300 Esc. (1997 values).

SOLEXPRESSO operates daily buses from Lisbon to the Algarve and to Elvas. The bus terminal is at Rua de Entrecampos, 1, near Campo Pequeno.

SANTOS runs daily buses from Lisbon and Oporto to Bragança and Miranda do Douro. Price: 2400 Esc. (in 1997) The terminal is at Campo das Cebolas, near Praça do Comércio.

# STAYING IN PORTUGAL

*Accommodation*

Accommodation is widely available in Portugal and a range of hotels exists to suit all pockets. Large hotels are usually restricted to the main cities. Small hotels (Estalagem, Albergaria, Residencial) are also available in many towns. In the very remote inland areas there may be only one or two small pensions (pensões) which are usually modest, but clean and not expensive. The coastal areas are the most important tourist attractions and there is a plethora of possibilities, from camping sites and pensions to five-star hotels. However, in July and August all the hotels may be fully booked because many Portuguese spend their summer holidays at the beach.

The 'pousadas' form a network of small to medium-sized hotels in some of the most beautiful parts of the country. There are about 40 pousadas in all, some of them close to sites described in this book, particularly at Gerês, Miranda do Douro, Marvão, Setúbal, Elvas, Évora and Sagres. The service is excellent, the food outstanding and the accommodation comfortable, although quite expensive.

If staying at smaller more modest hotels, it is advisable to 'shop around' before deciding on a particular hotel. The tourist office in every town will be happy to help you with maps, brochures and lists of seasonal events.

*Food*

From the gastronomical point of view, Portugal is relatively poorly known but is extremely interesting. Most regions have their own typical dishes and while it is not possible to describe them in detail here, visitors are encouraged to experiment with Portuguese food. It is advisable to purchase a small gastronomical pocket guide. A 'dose' (portion) of any typical dish is likely to shock you by its size and quantity and in many places you can request a 'meia-dose' (half-portion) which many people find quite sufficient.

Restaurants are to be found all over the country and most localities have their own typical restaurant, where tourists are particularly welcome, traditional dishes are served and waiters are extremely helpful. Although the opening times vary, meals are usually served from 12.00 to 15.00 hrs and from 19.00 to 23.00 hrs.

'Cafés' are probably more widespread in Portugal than anywhere else in Europe and are open from early morning to 22.00 hrs or even midnight. Here you may eat a sandwich or a small cake and drink juice, a glass of milk or a coffee at any time of the day. There are often chairs available to sit outside. These cafés may be found even in tiny villages. Spend some time resting at these oases – the local people can be as interesting as the birds!

Finally, there are small to large supermarkets all over the country, where a wide variety of food may be purchased. They are normally open from 09.00 to 20.00 hrs on weekdays and sometimes on weekends.

*Wine*

Portugal's wines are famed far beyond its frontiers and should be sampled by anyone visiting the country. Apart from the renowned Port, there are numerous excellent wines from every part of Portugal. In the northern part of the country, Vinho Verde is a unique treat and should be tasted there as it does not 'travel' well. In the centre, the best wines are certainly Dão and Bairrada, while in the more southerly and drier Alentejo the best known labels include Borba, Redondo and Reguengos.

However, remember that alcohol is still one of the main causes of road accidents in Portugal so if you drink (even moderately) *do not drive*. The law considers driving while drunk a major offence. It is also worth remembering that the heat plus 'one too many' may make you sleepy and end your birding forever! The blood alcohol limit is 0.5 g/l.

## Safety and thefts

In terms of personal safety, Portugal is widely regarded as less dangerous than many other southern European countries and, until recently, Lisbon was regarded as the safest European capital. Unfortunately, as in so many other cities today, crime has increased markedly in the last few years, especially drugs-related crime. It is therefore necessary to be sensible, especially within a radius of 50km of Lisbon, in most large cities and in the Algarve. Do not leave valuables in your car. If you must do so, conceal them well *before* parking your car. Car radios are stolen very frequently. Avoid carrying too much money at a time or in the same pocket.

In the more remote countryside, crime is much less of a problem. You may be asked what you are doing; common courtesy, mime and a bird book will usually suffice to persuade the enquirer that you are merely another mad 'forasteiro' (someone not from the local area).

## Cattle

*This warning is not to be taken lightly.*

Cattle farming forms an important component of agricultural activities in Portugal. Bull fights are almost as popular here as they are in Spain and these huge black fighting beasts wander freely in many areas of farmland, which, theoretically, are fully-fenced. Some of the areas described in this book are used for cattle grazing and extreme care is advisable. When driving on farm tracks, you may occasionally find our way blocked by wire gates. These gates are normally used to stop cattle moving from one field into the next. If the gates are not locked, there should be no problem in opening them and driving through. However, please close them immediately, as the bulls may escape and on return you might have to face an angry owner or an even angrier bull. Not all bulls may be recognisable as such, so be extra vigilant. When driving in areas with cattle (particularly in the Tagus Estuary), avoid jumping over fences and passing close to bulls.

It is also common to find the road blocked by a flock of sheep crossing or simply walking along the road, even in the middle of villages. Be patient and take care, even if the animals are occupying the whole width of the road; those few minutes of pastoral bliss may bring some high-flying raptor into view!

## Hunting

Hunting activities in Portugal reflect an ancient tradition once found throughout Europe and are an established pastime in Portuguese society. Although officially there are 300,000 registered hunters, there are also many illegal ones.

The list of birds that can be legally killed is unfortunately long. According to the law, hunting may only occur on Thursdays, Sundays and public holidays, between early October and late February (ducks, Turtle Dove and Quail may be shot as early as mid-August).

Conservation problems caused by overshooting are common, not only because of the excessively large number of hunters, but also because many of them do not respect the rules concerning sites, days, number of animals shot and species to be hunted. It is not uncommon to see a dead Red-crested Pochard dangling from a belt, injured or even stuffed birds of prey, mist-netted passerines being sold in markets as delicacies for restaurants, hunters claiming proudly to have shot an Eagle Owl, dozens of spent cartridges in fully-protected nature reserves, and so on.

For many years, following the 1974 revolution, hunting was a free-for-all event, the so-called 'Free regime', since nobody had to pay for shooting at a specific site, private or not. Recently new private hunting areas have been created and the operating rules are determined by a new law, which aims at bringing some order to a previously anarchic activity. Unfortunately, this new 'regime' has not been well received by traditional hunters, who are now either asked for a fee or forbidden to enter those areas that, due to soil-related agricultural decline, have been quickly turned into private hunting areas. The so-called 'control of animals of prey' is a common practice in some areas, where many birds of prey are still illegally shot, in the name of 'species conservation' and several raptors have seriously declined in numbers in recent years.

Caution should be exercised when walking through areas where hunting is likely to occur – these areas are marked by rectangular red and white metal plates labelled 'Zona de Caça'.

*Fire*     Portugal is partially a Mediterranean country, where fire is a natural agent and hazard. During the 20th century, Portuguese forests have been subject to marked changes; the original cover of oaks has been largely destroyed and partly replaced by pine and eucalyptus plantations. However, the combination of the climate and the species chosen for plantation have turned these woods into powder kegs, particularly in summer.

In the last few years, enormous forests have been destroyed by fire and though there is no doubt that natural conditions have changed markedly and predispose these forests to fire, it has been clearly shown that most fires are set by arsonists. In many cases, these are people with economic interests at stake or those wishing to revenge themselves on land owners who now contest shooting on their land. Fire, as in southern France, has almost turned into a 'tradition' during the summer months (June to September) and the consequences have been dramatic. In 1992, for example, about 100,000 ha of woodland was burned (over 1% of Portugal's surface, about 6% of its wooded areas).

Large fires can block important roads, lead to delays in your journey, and can be life-threatening. The northern and central parts of Portugal are more wooded and, as such, are the most sensitive areas. Care should be taken with discarded cigarettes, broken glass and picnic fires in woodland (emergency phone number for fire 117).

# WEATHER AND CLOTHING

Portugal lies on the periphery of south-west Europe, with a long coastline and a climate dominated by the Azores subtropical anticyclone. Because it stretches through five degrees of latitude, weather varies markedly from north to south, with a mild Atlantic regime obvious in the north-west and a distinctive Mediterranean type of climate elsewhere. The interior of Portugal experiences hot summers and cool winters and is characterised by a continental climatic regime, a feature compounded by the proximity of Spain's high meseta.

In the south the climate is basically Mediterranean, which calls for light clothes with a pullover for cooler evenings. Obviously early morning seawatches and walks through thorny scrub require warmer and more durable clothing respectively. Winters in the south may be wet and chilly and rainproof gear may be needed. Surprisingly perhaps, the Alentejo, known more for its hot dry summers, can suffer periods of cold weather in the winter. Pack clothing to suit these conditions.

In the north-west, the climate basically resembles that of southern Britain; equally British, the weather in this part of Portugal is notoriously unpredictable and clothing should be chosen accordingly.

In the north-east, around Bragança, summers may be extremely hot and winter temperatures may drop well below zero, when it is essential to wear warm and waterproof clothing. Remember that this area is like any other montane region – subject to sudden changes in weather. Be careful to check weather forecasts before setting out to walk across the mountain tops.

# HEALTH AND MEDICAL FACILITIES

As in most of Europe, the chance of contracting a serious infectious disease in Portugal is remote.

It is not necessary to be vaccinated against any major diseases and the worst problem you may encounter is likely to be mild diarrhoea or sunburn.

Tapwater is perfectly safe to drink almost everywhere, but it may be distasteful. Bottled water is an excellent and cheap alternative. Always carry a supply of water, especially in summer. Like everywhere that is seasonally warm, there is a slightly heightened risk of eating food that may cause gastro-enteritis. If you do get diarrhoea, Imodium (available in all pharmacies), is a good remedy (opening time of pharmacies 09.00 to 19.00; in any area one of them stays open all night for emergencies). Obviously persistent symptoms should not be ignored and you should consult a doctor (médico)

Sunburn (and even sunstroke) should be taken seriously, not only because it may spoil your trip but because serious burns can have dangerous consequences. Always wear a hat, even in winter; use strong barrier creams, especially if you are light-skinned, and avoid exposure to the sun between 12.00 and 16.00 hrs in summer.

Problems with snakebites are very, very rare but obviously if bitten it is essential to obtain medical assistance as soon as possible. Scorpions do exist but the risk of being stung is minimal. A mosquito repellent is useful in summer. Those containing deet (diethyltoluamide) are the most effective, but concern has been expressed about their long-term effect on the skin. A suitable alternative that works reasonably well is Mosi-guard Natural, produced by MASTA, which is available from most larger high street pharmacies (farmácia).

There are hospitals all over the country but as elsewhere the most comprehensive medical care is available only in the larger cities. It is usually not difficult to find a doctor and pharmacies are widespread.

E.U. citizens should carry form E111 from their home country. It entitles them to free hospital treatment. It is advisable to take out some form of medical insurance even for short periods. Ensure that your travel insurance covers both medical costs and repatriation in case of need.

If an emergency arises, 112 is the national emergency number, both from fixed and from mobile telephones.

# MAPS

To get the best out of this book, a general map of the country should be purchased to identify the different roads mentioned and to locate the principal towns and cities. There are many large-scale maps (1:300,000 to 1:400,000) available, though the following ones are especially recommended:

- Automóvel Club de Portugal, scale 1:350,000 (available in bookshops or directly from A.C.P., at Rua Rosa Araújo, 24, in Lisbon).
- Michelin map no. 440 (Portugal), scale 1:400,000.

For many sites, however, a more detailed map is invaluable to reach specific places. It is possible to purchase small-scale maps for any part of the country and the following scales are available:

1:100,000; 1:50,000 and 1:25,000.

Maps of the first two scales can be purchased at Instituto Português de Cartografia e Cadastro, Rua Artilharia 1, 107 (near Amoreiras Shopping Centre). Ask for the 'Venda de Cartas' (Map sales section). It is open from 09.00 to 16.00 hrs and as of 1997 the maps cost 1000 Esc. each (you may be asked for identification at entrance).

The 1:25,000 maps are a military edition and can be obtained from Instituto Geográfico do Exército, Avenida Dr. Alfredo Bensaúde, in Lisbon. To get there, leave Lisbon city centre following signs to the airport. On reaching the large roundabout which is just 500m before the airport, follow the signs to A1 and Oporto and proceed for about 1.5km, turning right after the GALP petrol station. Continuing along a wide avenue for about 500m, one reaches a large building on the left, called Instituto Geográfico do Exército. Enter and ask for the 'Venda de Cartas' (Map Sales Section). It is open from 09.00 to 16.30 hrs and the unit price as of 1997 is 1000 Esc. (identification may be necessary to enter the building).

The best source of maps in the United Kingdom is probably Stanford's International Map Centre, 12-14 Long Acre, Covent Garden, London, WC2E 9LP (Tel: 0171 836 1321).

To facilitate identification of the best small scale map to be purchased for each of the main sites in this book, the corresponding number is given at the beginning of each site description.

# GEOGRAPHY AND VEGETATION

Portugal is a quadrilateral of land occupying the western coast of Iberia, stretching from 36°58′ N to 42°09′ N. A little under half of the land area lies below 200m. In terms of physical geography there are several distinct regions: the montane areas of the north, the eastern plains, the basins of the Tagus and Sado rivers, and the peripheral western and southern borders. These areas, each with its own distinct avifauna, have been moulded by three factors: a seismically active underlying structure, the rock type, and the climate. Leaving aside the tectonic aspects for which Portugal is famous (or infamous, depending upon how you view the Great Lisbon Earthquake of 1755), there are three rock types that fundamentally affect the landscape and vegetation: calcareous, granitic and schistose.

The calcareous limestone areas have the distinct and beautiful morphology of karst, well seen in the Estremadura ranges of west-central Portugal (e.g. Serra da Arrábida). Relief underlain by granite is widespread in the north and forms the rather spectacular scenery of Serras da Estrela, Sintra and part of the eastern Alentejo. The gradients are steep, giving deep valleys, cascades and water falls. Rivers crossing it tend to produce characteristic 'dog-leg' turns as they follow the fracture lines of the granite. The classic steppe landscape of the Alentejo with its rolling rounded hillocks, long vistas and fields of Little Bustards and larks is underlain by schistose rock. The few rivers that wander across this peneplain do so in long, wide, shallow valleys like that of the Sado. In the Beira areas the schist produces a more contrasting landscape with deep cut valleys and high river banks ideal for hole nesting birds.

Past climates both cold and hot have left tangible marks upon the landscape of Portugal from the ruddy soil of bauxite deposits to the glaciated U-shaped valley of the Zêzere river in the Serra da Estrela. On a hot day in July it is difficult to appreciate that this valley is one of the best examples of its kind in the world.

Portugal's coastline, an ancient abraded continental platform is marked by its regular outline. The long sweeps of sand and dune are broken, occasionally spectacularly, by capes such as Cape da Roca and estuaries such as the Tagus. Sand banks and spits are common and together with slow uplift have produced the lagoons and marshland so characteristic of Aveiro, Faro and Santo André.

The vegetation of Portugal just before man's intervention was dominated by oak species, deciduous in the cooler wetter north, evergreen in the warmer drier south. This pattern still persists, though much modified by man and local mesoclimatic effects. Portuguese oak woods are characteristically complex and diversified, with a wide variation in avifauna. In the north-west the dominant tree is Pedunculate Oak (*Quercus robur*), while in the higher reaches of the north-east, Pyrenean Oak (*Q. pyrenaica*) is more common. In the south and in the east-north-east, the oak woods consist almost entirely of evergreen oaks such as Holm Oak (*Q. rotundifolia*). In the west-central

fringes Lusitanian Oak (*Q. faginea*) can be found and, south of the
Tagus, Cork Oak (*Q. suber*) and Holm Oak are increasingly the two only
large oaks to be found. Over the past 150 years widespread
replacement of these oak groves has taken place. Plantations of
Maritime Pine (*Pinus pinaster*) have displaced the old Pyrenean Oak
and Lusitanian Oak forests. Plantation management and a resultant
lowering of the water table have combined to degrade the soil in large
areas of Portugal and officially over 80% of Portugal's soils are under
some form of stress. Umbrella Pines (*Pinus pinea*) occur mainly in the
Sado basin. Holm Oak woods have largely disappeared under a swathe
of wheat in Beira Baixa, Alentejo and the Algarve hills. Loss of the
understorey vegetation to secondary formations has lead to
environmental degradation, while vast plantations of eucalyptus trees
(*Eucalyptus globulus* and other species) in areas of fragile, friable soil
have eliminated many natural springs, removed top soil and reduced
biodiversity. Much of the native flora of the Algarve has been replaced
by orchard species though Olive (*Olea europaea*), carob (*Ceratonia sp.*),
Almond (*Prunus dulcis*) and Fig (*Ficus carica*) still abound and offer
excellent habitat for both breeding and migrant birds.

Fire and grazing have also taken their toll with oak groves
successively reduced to thickets of maquis with Tree Heather (*Erica
arborea*), pistachio (*Pistacia sp.*) and Strawberry Tree (*Arbutus unedo*).
Further loss of biodiversity has lead to the spread of dense areas of
garrigue (thorny low growing dense vegetation) – dominated by the
small Kermes Oak (*Quercus coccifera*). It has also lead to hillsides being
swathed in monotonous swards of spiny scrub plants such as gorse
(*Ulex sp.*), heather (*Erica sp.*) and sun rose (*Cistus sp.*).

# WHEN TO GO

For breeding birds, March to June is best and is the most pleasant season generally. Passage migrants can be best found in March and April. Mid summer can be unpleasantly hot and overcrowded at the coast. Autumn passage begins in early August and birds are still on the move in mid November, by which time the weather may be wet and windy. Winter, though wet is usually mild and can produce interesting and unexpected species, especially water birds. Thus, from the ornithological point of view, Portugal is interesting all year round.

*Breeding birds*

The north-west of Portugal is a mixture of Atlantic influences and continental effects both in its climate and in its vegetation. Some northern species are at their southern limit in this area and these include Tree Pipit, Whinchat, Red-backed Shrike and Yellowhammer. The range of birds of prey breeding includes Montagu's Harrier, Honey Buzzard and Golden Eagle.

In the north-eastern part of Portugal, the Douro forms the frontier with Spain. It is a remarkable area, with breeding White and Black Storks, Griffon and Egyptian Vultures, Red and Black Kites, and Short-toed, Booted, Bonelli's and Golden Eagles. Scops Owls are common summer visitors and Eagle Owls may be heard from January onwards in suitable habitat. Other breeding species are numerous and include many of those most sought-after, such as Red-necked Nightjar, Wryneck and Orphean Warbler. In spring Subalpine, Bonelli's and Melodious Warblers, Golden Orioles, and Rock Buntings seem to be everywhere.

Moving southwards and with the Tagus forming the frontier between Spain and Portugal, one enters one of the most spectacular areas for raptors and vultures with resident Griffon and Black Vultures, Golden Eagle, Black-shouldered Kite and Eagle Owl. On the plains, the classic suite of steppe birds can be found, from Little Bustard to Calandra Lark. If Pin-tailed Sandgrouse still exists in Portugal, this is probably where it will be relocated.

Following the Tagus as it enters Portugal, one reaches Boquilobo Marsh near Golegã, one of the best wetlands for breeding herons and egrets in the country. Whiskered Tern breeds here, though nest sites often disappear in the dust of summer.

About 100km south lies Lisbon, on the enormous estuary of the Tagus, and a little further south the Sado enters the sea at Setúbal. Though more famous for their passage and wintering water birds, both these estuaries can boast a good cross-section of southern Europe's most interesting summer visitors, including Collared Pratincole, Bee-eater and Short-toed Lark. A large heronry lies on the southern bank of the Sado.

South east of Lisbon, across the Tagus, lie the plains and hills of the Alentejo. In the east, the famed steppe occurs, but agro-business is slowly destroying this habitat. Nevertheless Stone-curlews and Little Bustards breed and a wide variety of summer passerines occur. Close to the Spanish border Black-bellied Sandgrouse can still be found, and in some areas vultures and other soaring raptors are a common sight. Indeed the catchment of the Guadiana in Portugal proper is still a unique area, with breeding Lesser Kestrel, Great Bustard, Rufous

Bushchat, Spectacled Warbler and Spanish Sparrow.

The Algarve holds a wide variety of breeding species, but little by little the habitat is being altered or buried under concrete. The Ria Formosa and Castro Marim hold breeding waders and six species of larks breed within the boundaries of the latter reserve. Fortunately, the Algarve with its 'barrocal' (a fertile limestone hinterland with orchards, allotments and many Fig and Carob trees) and its maquis vegetation is still attractive to a wide range of southern European summer visitors, including Golden Oriole, Woodchat Shrike and Red-necked Nightjar.

*Migrants and winter visitors*

Most winter visitors arrive from August onwards and many have departed by late March. Divers are scarce to rare, but Cormorants become numerous and Greylag Geese appear in the Tagus. Wildfowl numbers peak in January; the Tagus Estuary at this time and can hold tens of thousands of ducks and shorebirds – interesting wintering waders include Avocet, Little Stint, Black-winged Stilt and Ruff. Cranes winter in some numbers in the east of the country, sometimes in the same fields as Great Bustard and Black-bellied Sandgrouse.

In winter, Sandwich Terns, Mediterranean Gulls and enormous flocks of Lesser Black-backed Gulls fill the estuaries. Large numbers of Skylarks, Meadow and Water Pipits, and Bluethroats winter in Portugal, the last named mainly in coastal saltmarsh. Among the winter thrushes, Redwings are common, but Fieldfares seem to be scarce. Finches and buntings winter in large numbers and sometimes flocks of Bramblings, Siskins and Crossbills arrive with them.

As is the case throughout temperate and Southern Europe, it is sometimes difficult to distinguish between passage migrants and winter visitors, as the same species may utilise both strategies. It is even more difficult to tell whether a trans-Saharan migrant is about to breed or is on passage, with White Storks occupying nests in January, Great Spotted Cuckoos in February actively courting and Flamingos all year round in the largest wetlands.

Of those species that do not breed in Portugal or do so only in tiny numbers, the passage migration of waders is probably the most spectacular. Northward movement peaks in April and May and can include vast flocks of Black-tailed Godwits, Grey Plovers and Knot flying over estuarine areas or north along the coast. Offshore, Great and Arctic Skuas appear, sometimes in large numbers, flying north after wintering in Portuguese waters, though spring sightings of Pomarine and Long-tailed Skuas are rare. Common and Black Terns pass north from April onwards and occasionally heavy passage is still obvious in May.

Among the passerines, some passage migrants are instantly recognisable such as *flavissima* and *thunbergi* Yellow Wagtails that pass north in April and early May. Sedge and Willow Warblers are often numerous on passage from late March, singing as they go. It can be puzzling to hear Sedge, Reed, Great Reed and Savi's Warblers all singing in the same tiny patch of reeds. However, it is clear that spring migration is a rapid and well-timed event which in Iberia takes place far to the east of Portugal.

In autumn, most passage migrants in Portugal are adults in winter plumage or immatures in first-winter plumage and can provide a real identification challenge. Storm-driven seabirds may pass south in spectacular numbers, and raptors can be seen circling southwards at some headlands in good numbers. Sightings of migrants often depend on weather conditions, but in general the numbers of migrants in autumn are far greater than in spring. Late November marks the end of most active migration. However, seawatching may reveal heavy movements of seabirds, especially of auks and Gannets, well into December. In some autumns, Great Skuas may pass southwards in thousands, an awesome sight as party upon party move purposefully low over the sea within metres of the shore.

# MAIN SITES

Note that in the description of the various sites it is assumed that most readers will be aware of seasonal changes in birds species and that when a summer visitor is mentioned it means that the bird is to be seen in the appropriate season. In case of doubt about the status of any species, it is a simple matter to consult the lists and tables provided at the end of the book.

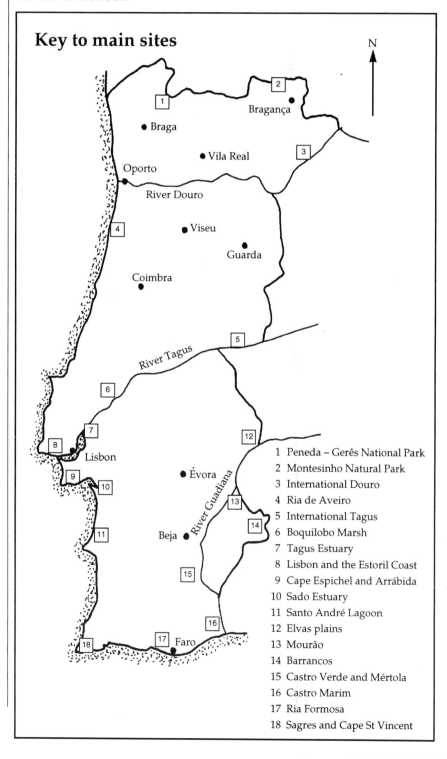

**Key to main sites**

N

Bragança

Braga

Vila Real

Oporto

River Douro

Viseu

Guarda

Coimbra

River Tagus

Lisbon

Évora

River Guadiana

Beja

Faro

1 Peneda – Gerês National Park
2 Montesinho Natural Park
3 International Douro
4 Ria de Aveiro
5 International Tagus
6 Boquilobo Marsh
7 Tagus Estuary
8 Lisbon and the Estoril Coast
9 Cape Espichel and Arrábida
10 Sado Estuary
11 Santo André Lagoon
12 Elvas plains
13 Mourão
14 Barrancos
15 Castro Verde and Mértola
16 Castro Marim
17 Ria Formosa
18 Sagres and Cape St Vincent

# 1 Peneda-Gerês National Park

This is the only National Park in Portugal. It extends over several mountain ranges and is particularly important for its large and medium-sized mammals, which include Wolf and Roe Deer. This is a region influenced by a moist air stream off the Atlantic, with the highest rainfall in Portugal. Disturbance has increased over the last fifteen years, mainly due to tourism and to the disastrous fires which have lead to the destruction of large areas of the park. The bird life is dominated by passerines and many northern species reach their southern limits here.

*Location*

The park lies in the north-western corner of the country to the north-east of the town of Braga, which lies 50km north-east of Oporto. Full details of the area can be found on the following maps: 1:100,000: 1, 2, 5, and 6; 1:50,000: 1-B, 1-D, 2-C, 5-B, and 6-A; 1:25,000: 4, 5, 9, 17, 18, 19, 30, 31, and 32.

*Description*

This is a medium to high altitude region (500 to over 1500m), extending over several chains of hills (serras): Peneda, Soajo, Amarela and Gerês. Despite the proximity of the Atlantic, the temperature range is extreme because of altitude, resulting in warm summers and cold, often snowy, winters. There are some villages scattered throughout the area, although the most remote parts are uninhabited. On the higher hills there is little vegetation and the soil is often bare or simply covered with low scrub, while at lower altitudes there are wooded areas, consisting mainly of Pedunculate Oak and Maritime Pine, with a few Pyrenean Oaks, Birch, Scots Pine and Ash Trees in some places.

*Birds*

The common interesting breeding birds include Quail, Hoopoe, Woodlark, Black Redstart, Bonelli's and Dartford Warblers, Firecrest, Short-toed Treecreeper, Golden Oriole, Red-backed Shrike, Serin and Rock Bunting. Other species, not so common, but still to be found in suitable habitat include Scops Owl, European Nightjar, Crag Martin, Fan-tailed Warbler, Crested Tit, Southern Grey Shrike, Chough, and Cirl and Ortolan Buntings. The open mountain tops hold Rock Thrush, along with Tawny Pipit and Wheatear.

This area forms the Portuguese stronghold of several 'northern' species, like Tree Pipit, Whinchat, Song Thrush, Garden Warbler, Bullfinch, Crossbill (irregular) and Yellowhammer.

The most common birds of prey include Buzzard, Montagu's Harrier (a proportion of which are all-dark morphs) and Sparrowhawk. Less common raptors include Black Kite, Honey Buzzard, Hen Harrier, Goshawk, Short-toed and Golden Eagles, and Peregrine.

In the colder months the summer visitors are absent and many resident species undertake altitudinal movements, thus avoiding the harsh conditions. At that time of year, the area has much less to offer. Nevertheless, Alpine Accentor and Water Pipit have been recorded in winter.

Finding a place to stay should not be a problem. At Gerês village there are several hotels and a camp site, while near the Vilarinho das Furnas dam there is a youth hostel. The Pousada de São Bento, a few km to the south of Gerês village, provides excellent views over the valleys. Another possibility is to use the mountain huts that exist all over the park, but it is necessary to book them well in advance (please contact the park headquarters in Braga; see p 141). Finally there are small pensions in Castro Laboreiro or Melgaço.

There are many restaurants in the area, including some at Gerês village, Covelães, Pitões das Júnias and Tourém, as well as at Montalegre, which lies further east.

The best season for visiting the area is from April to August, when most breeding species are present. Because of the large area concerned, strategy has been divided into two sections.

**a) Central and eastern sectors (Serra do Gerês)**

Serra do Gerês is best reached from the town of Braga. Take the N103 signposted to Chaves, which leads to Pisões (after 75km). Turn left on a small road just after Pisões, towards Covelães.

Start by exploring the area just before Covelães, which includes the road that leads westwards to Outeiro and Paradela. Interesting species to be found here include Honey Buzzard, Goshawk, Scops Owl, European Nightjar, Bonelli's Warbler, Golden Oriole and Rock Bunting.

After Covelães, continue northwards, stopping after 2km where the wooded areas give way to more open country. This is a good area for Montagu's Harrier, Short-toed Eagle, Southern Grey and Red-backed Shrikes, Chough, and Ortolan Bunting. A few kilometres further north, the road forks. Take the left fork to Pitões das Júnias. Park and ask for the 'Convento' (the old medieval convent), which can be reached in a 20 minute walk. Birds along the way may include Short-toed Eagle, Scops Owl, Bonelli's Warbler, Red-backed Shrike and Rock Bunting. A walk further down to the waterfall sometimes produces Dipper.

From Pitões das Júnias, there is an unsurfaced road that leads north-west towards Fonte Fria. Drive for a few kilometres, stop where the road ends and walk on in the same direction through some woods to the open tops. Montagu's Harriers, Bonelli's and Dartford Warblers and Rock Thrush are all possible here.

Return to Pitões das Júnias, drive back to the fork and take the left road to Tourém, which goes through the plateau, locally called Planalto da Mourela. Breeding birds include Quail, Tawny Pipit, Golden Oriole and Ortolan Bunting. Red-backed Shrikes are common on the telephone wires here from mid-May onwards. Birds of prey include Short-toed and Golden Eagles, Montagu's Harriers and Honey Buzzard. It is worth carrying on towards the Spanish border, beyond Tourém. Black Redstart breeds in the village and Crag Martin under the bridge immediately outside the village, while Scops Owl and Iberian Yellow Wagtail occur nearby.

Another interesting area lies between Gerês village and Portela do Homem. To get there, leave the N103 near the Pousada de São Bento and proceed through Gerês village on the N308-1 northwards to Albergaria, where there is a large wood. Here it is possible to find Goshawk, Montagu's Harrier, Scops Owl, Dipper and Iberian Chiffchaff, among others.

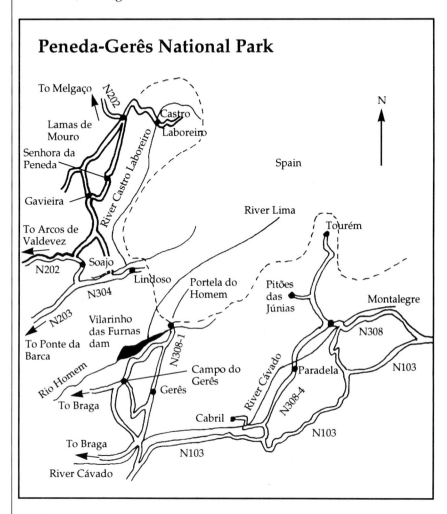

**Peneda-Gerês National Park**

### b) North-western part (Serra da Peneda)

From Braga take the N101 north to Ponte da Barca and then turn east on a minor road to Soajo (where the typical corn storage 'Espigueiros' should not be missed). From Soajo, an unsurfaced road leads northwards to Senhora da Peneda and then on to Lamas de Mouro and Castro Laboreiro. Alternatively, take the N101 to Monção and then follow the N202 through Melgaço to Castro Laboreiro.

Once at the village of Castro Laboreiro, park the car and explore the plateau and the oak woods on foot. The most interesting species to be found here include Scops Owl, Rock Thrush and Ortolan Bunting. Other species occurring in the area include Montagu's Harrier, Short-toed and Golden Eagles, European Nightjar, Woodlark, Tawny Pipit, Dipper, Melodious and Bonelli's Warblers, Firecrest, Crested Tit, Golden Oriole, and Red-backed Shrike.

# 2 Montesinho Natural Park

Many central and northern European species reach their southern limit in Montesinho Natural Park, yet there are also many Mediterranean species present and the result is a remarkable mixed bird community. The park is in a mountainous area, which is hot in summer and very cold in winter. Human activities are mainly agricultural and there are no large centres of population in the park; for visiting birdwatchers passerines are of most interest.

*Location*

Montesinho Natural Park is situated in the north-eastern corner of Portugal, close to Bragança. The park's northern, western and eastern boundaries are formed by the Spanish border. The southern boundary is formed by the N103 (west of Bragança) and by the N218 and N218-1, which run from Bragança eastwards to Quintanilha. Full details of the area can be found on the following maps: 1:100,000: 3, 4 and 8; 1:50,000: 3-C, 3-D, 4-C and 8-A; 1:25,000: 10, 11, 12, 13, 23, 24, 25, 26, and 39.

*Description*

The landscape is varied, complex and hilly, with most of the park at an altitude of over 700m. There are many different intergraded habitats, which occur throughout the area. The more open locations consist of cultivated and uncultivated plots, and occur especially in the eastern half of the park. There are many grassy fields, mainly used for grazing and pasture, which are divided by small stone walls or bushy hedges. These fields, locally called 'lameiros', are often surrounded by Ash trees, Pyrenean Oak, Poplars and Birch.

Woodland is an important habitat here, although much has been cleared. The park holds important groves of Pyrenean Oak, which originally covered almost the whole area, but are nowadays almost restricted to those places which have not yet been transformed. They are most frequent in the western and central half of the park. Many areas have been planted with a variety of pine species (Maritime Pine, Scots Pine and Corsican Pine) and Douglas Fir. There are also many plantations of sweet chestnut, a species with a relatively high ecological rating in terms of associated biodiversity. Elms occur mainly in inhabited areas and along watercourses and roads. Unfortunately, practically all the Elms have died out in recent years, the result of a disease that affected Iberia, along with many other European regions.

*Birds*

Passerines are undoubtedly the most interesting bird group to look for in this area. Common and widespread breeding species, which can be seen almost anywhere in the park include Tawny Pipit, Subalpine, Bonelli's, Melodious and Dartford Warblers, Iberian Chiffchaff, Short-toed Treecreeper, Golden Oriole, Spotless Starling, Serin, and Cirl and Rock Buntings. Wrynecks are fairly common all over the park and are best located in April and May, when their song is heard most frequently, usually in old chestnut woods.

Less common species, which are rather more habitat dependent are: Quail, Bee-eater, Short-toed Lark, Black-eared Wheatear, and Fan-tailed

Warbler in more open habitats; Red-rumped Swallow, Dipper and Blue Rock Thrush in deep river valleys; Redstart and Rock Sparrow in chestnut woods; Rock Thrush in the higher mountainous areas. Water Pipit has bred here on the high ranges and can be seen in winter in small numbers. Crossbills occur in some years and may breed at times, mainly after irruptive years in northern or eastern Europe, and are usually seen in Scots Pine forest.

Birds of prey are not numerous. The only two common species are Buzzard and Montagu's Harrier. Rarer birds, which are more difficult to locate, include Golden and Short-toed Eagles, Goshawk, Sparrowhawk, Red and Black Kites and Egyptian Vultures. About 20 pairs of White Stork breed here, as well as a pair of Black Storks.

Among the night birds, Scops is by far the most common owl and is easy to hear in the breeding season. Eagle Owl is very rare and finding one requires luck and patience; it begins its breeding cycle and thus its lugubrious song in early January. There are also European and Red-necked Nightjars, although the latter reaches its northernmost limit here and is very scarce north of Bragança.

In winter the area is very cold and snow-covered, and birds are not numerous.

*Accommodation*

Bragança is the most convenient town in which to be based and there are several pensions and hotels to choose from. There are a few mountain huts scattered within the park that may be available through the park headquarters at Bragança (see p 141). It will be necessary to supply your own food, water and bedding.

There are a few restaurants in the towns of Bragança and Vinhais and in the village of Gimonde.

*Strategy*

April to July is the best time to visit the park. Access may be time consuming and two or three days may be necessary to explore the area thoroughly. A detailed map can be very useful. In terms of strategy, the park can roughly be divided into three areas, based on access rather than birds.

**a) Eastern sector**

The easternmost area can be explored by leaving Bragança eastwards on the N218. After 4km, stop at Gimonde. Look for Crag Martin and Red-rumped Swallow, which breed under the bridge. A breeding pair of White Storks, Melodious Warblers and Woodchat Shrikes occur nearby.

Proceed along the N308, until São Julião or Deilão is reached. This is an open, cultivated area, which is best explored on foot. Breeding species here include Short-toed Eagle, Quail, Great Spotted Cuckoo, Bee-eater, Wryneck, Short-toed and Thekla Larks, Woodlark, Black-eared Wheatear, Bonelli's Warbler, and Ortolan Bunting. Slightly further north, there are plantations of Scots Pine, where Crossbills are seen occasionally. Further south, near Quintanilha, explore the valley of the River Maçãs where there are regular sightings of Egyptian Vulture, Goshawk, Crag Martin, Black-eared Wheatear, and Cetti's Warbler.

### b) Central sector

The central sector includes some montane locations, such as Serra de Montesinho, which are excellent for high altitude species. From Bragança, drive north on the N103-7. Pass França and just before Portelo turn left to Montesinho. The road runs upwards and leads to a cross-roads.

Continue straight through proceeding downwards until Montesinho village is reached; it lies in the bottom of a valley, at about 900m. The surrounding area, although highly agricultural, is very beautiful and is peppered with small woodlands of oak and birch. This area holds a variety of birds, including Golden Eagle, Wryneck, Woodlark, Crag Martin, Tawny Pipit, Bonelli's Warbler, Iberian Chiffchaff and Red-backed Shrike.

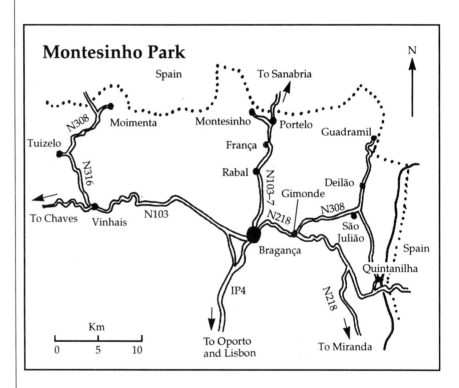

If you turn right at the cross-roads mentioned above, you can proceed on an unsurfaced but negotiable road leading upwards to an almost treeless plateau at about 1300m, where there is a reservoir (Serra Serrada dam). Interesting birds here include Golden Eagle, Tawny Pipit, Rock Thrush, Red-backed Shrike, and Ortolan Bunting. After a few more kilometres the road reaches the highest part of the park (over 1450m), which consists of high altitude pastureland and scrub, with a few birch trees. The variety of birds is smaller here, but there are some specialities, including Hen and Montagu's Harriers, Rock Thrush, Southern Grey and Red-backed Shrikes and possibly the only breeding Water Pipits in the country. Tawny Pipit and Dartford Warbler are common here while Water Pipit is common in winter.

**c) Western sector**

Leave Bragança westwards on the N103 to Vinhais. From here, a few roads lead into the park, which are all worth exploring. The best area however lies around Moimenta (25km to the north), near the international road to Orense (Spain). It consists of a plateau where agricultural areas alternate with woods, pastures and scrub. Park the car near the village and explore the surrounding areas on foot. There is an enormous variety of breeding birds here, including Honey Buzzard, Montagu's Harrier, European Nightjar, Bee-eater, Wryneck, Short-toed Lark, Woodlark, Tawny Pipit, Bonelli's Warbler, Red-backed Shrike, Golden Oriole and Ortolan Bunting.

# 3 International Douro

In the north-eastern corner of Portugal, the River Douro runs through a deep rocky valley. Apart from several dams that have been built there, the entire area is relatively unspoiled and, although it is not protected, there are plans to create a natural park here. The area is of particular interest for its birds of prey, its vultures and for several species favouring rocky habitats.

*Location*

The River Douro runs across the northern part of Portugal from Spain to Oporto and the eastern part, which forms the border between the two countries, is known as International Douro. Full details of the area can be found on the following maps: 1:100,000: 8, 11, 12 and 15; 1:50,000: 8-C, 11-B, 11-D, 12-A, 12-C and 15-B; 1:25,000: 67, 81, 94, 95, 107, 108, 120, 121, 131, 132, 142, 142A, 152 and 162.

The best way to reach the area from Lisbon is by car (the whole journey will take about 6 hours) or by bus (daily buses are run by SANTOS).

*Description*

The area extends along the valley of the Douro from Miranda do Douro to Barca d'Alva. Its core is the valley itself, which is wide, cliff-lined and scrub-covered in some places, lending to the whole landscape a dramatic natural beauty. There are five dams along the river, mainly used for energy production, which have weakened the water current throughout much of the area. There are few buildings on the shore line, and human disturbance is virtually absent (apart from the dams).

Away from the valley, the vegetation becomes heterogeneous with open areas, consisting mainly of small to medium-sized cultivated and uncultivated fields, alternating with small woods. The dominant trees are Maritime Pines and Holm Oaks, usually surrounded by Genista scrub.

Typical features of this region are the 'lameiros', small rectangular grassy fields (about 1 or 2ha in size), separated by small stone walls and mainly used for grazing. Pyrenean Oaks and Sweet Chestnut groves are more common around Mogadouro and north of Miranda do Douro and further south around Freixo de Espada à Cinta the wooded areas consist largely of Almond trees and Olive groves.

*Birds*   This is one of the best areas for raptors, vultures and Black Storks in the country. Breeding species include Griffon and Egyptian Vultures, Red and Black Kites, White and Black Storks, as well as Short-toed, Booted, Bonelli's and Golden Eagles. Owls include Scops Owl (numerous as a summer visitor) and Eagle Owl (still relatively common in suitable habitat).

There is an abundance of breeding birds during the summer. Nightingales, Subalpine Warblers and Golden Orioles seem to be everywhere; other common summer visitors or residents include Alpine Swift, Woodlark, Crag Martin, Red-rumped Swallow, Melodious and Bonelli's Warblers, Woodchat Shrike, Chough, Rock Sparrow, Hawfinch and Rock Bunting.

The area also holds some specialised or otherwise scarce species, including Great Spotted Cuckoo, European and Red-necked Nightjars, Roller, Wryneck, Blue Rock Thrush, Orphean Warbler, and Azure-winged Magpie.

*Accommodation*   Miranda do Douro is a convenient place to stay. It is a rather small town with few pensions and one 'pousada', all located near the centre. There is also a camp site near the town. 'Posta à Mirandesa', a very typical dish, should definitely be sampled as there are several good restaurants here. Further south, accommodation can be found at Mogadouro and at Freixo de Espada à Cinta.

*Strategy*   The best time to visit this area is between April and July. Remember it can be almost unpleasant in midsummer, because of the heat, especially between 12.00 and 16.00 hrs.

Egyptian and Griffon Vultures

This whole area is very remote, but the effort required to reach it is definitely worth while, as the bird life is so diverse and rich.

For convenience, the strategy is presented in three subsections.

### a) Miranda do Douro

This picturesque town lies close to where the River Douro enters the country. Since most birds can be seen within a short distance of the town, the most sensible strategy is to use the town as a base.

Start by exploring the town itself, with its beautiful monuments and splendid views over the river valley. Black Redstart, Spotless Starling and Rock Sparrow can be found in the cathedral tower or in the old castle; Crag Martin is regular in the dam wall just below the town, while Blue Rock Thrush occurs in the river valley. Golden Oriole occurs wherever there are trees, even close to the town. Bonelli's Eagles, Griffon and Egyptian Vultures, Red Kites and Alpine Swifts fly over frequently and birdwatching from your hotel window may be practical and rewarding.

To explore northwards, take the road to Ifanes and follow it for 3km, before taking a minor road to the right. This leads to Vale de Água. On arriving at this village, take one of the various tracks to the right that approach the river valley and explore on foot. This area consists mainly of large bushes and Holm Oaks, and it is possible to find Booted Eagle, Subalpine Warbler and Hawfinch here, while in the river valley Griffon and Egyptian Vultures, Golden Eagle, Red Kite, Alpine Swift, Crag Martin, Red-rumped Swallow and Chough all occur.

Returning to the road to Ifanes, proceed north and on reaching that village, veer eastwards to Paradela (the easternmost village in Portugal). On arriving at Paradela, take the furthest right fork which leads to the 'corner' of Portugal, where the River Douro enters the country. Here there are many uncultivated fields, as well as some Pyrenean Oak and Maritime Pine woods. Breeding species include Montagu's Harrier, Wryneck, Thekla, and Short-toed Larks, Woodlark, Crag Martin, Subalpine and Bonelli's Warblers and Hawfinch.

To the south of Miranda, the N221 is worth walking or driving for a few kilometres. A parallel track as far as Cércio is easier for walking. Here there are pine woods and the ubiquitous 'lameiros', together with some open fields, always close to the river valley. Here it is not difficult to find Black Stork, Egyptian Vulture, Golden Eagle, Bee-eater, Roller, Scops Owl, Golden Oriole, Orphean and Bonelli's Warblers, and Chough. Great Spotted Cuckoo has been seen in successive years just south of Sendim, which lies a few km further south.

Evening and dusk can be very rewarding, if the best sites are carefully and patiently explored. Red-necked Nightjars are often seen sitting on the avenues just outside of the wall that surrounds the old town, while European Nightjars have been heard near the river valley. It is difficult not to hear Scops Owls from April to June in the trees just outside the town wall. To locate Eagle Owl, choose a very rocky part of the valley, preferably after sunset. Remember that these birds are scarce and patience is needed to hear and, especially, to see them.

## b) Mogadouro

This town lies in the middle of a large plateau and access from it to the Douro valley is not easy as it lies well to the west of the river.

Starting from Mogadouro, take the N221 southwards, keeping an eye open for flying raptors: Red Kites, Griffon and Egyptian Vultures are often seen flying over the road and occasionally over Mogadouro town. After about 16km there is a minor road to the left that leads to Bruçó (signposted). This village is reached after 4km. Drive through the village and park the car. From here, it is possible to reach the river valley in a 20 min walk. This area is excellent for Black Stork, Vultures, Golden and Booted Eagles as well as for smaller, cliff-nesting birds such as Alpine Swift, Crag Martin, Red-rumped Swallow, Blue Rock Thrush and Chough. The Genista bushes on the way hold Dartford and Subalpine Warblers, while the Pyrenean Oaks along the road back to the N221 are worth exploring for Bonelli's Warbler and Golden Oriole.

Return to the N221 and drive for another 10km southwards until the

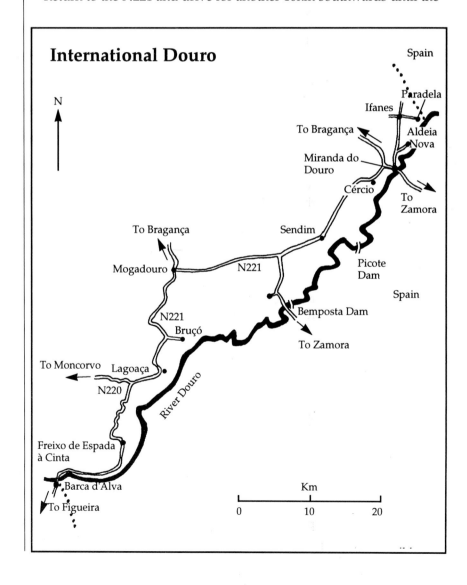

village of Lagoaça (signposted) is reached. It lies slightly off the main
road to the east, close to the shore of the Douro. Go through the village
and on reaching the graveyard ('cemitério' in Portuguese), take the
right fork and proceed for about 500m until the track ends at a
remarkable and breathtaking viewing point. Park the car and look for
flying vultures, eagles, kites and Black Stork, preferably around noon.
In the surrounding bushes and trees, Subalpine and Dartford Warblers,
Golden Oriole, and Rock Bunting can be found, while Bee-eaters and
Alpine Swifts are usually visible or audible overhead. Azure-winged
Magpies are at the northern limit of their range and have been seen
here.

If staying at Mogadouro town itself, it is worth taking a walk around
at dusk and listening for the characteristic calls of the Scops Owls.

### c) Freixo de Espada à Cinta

This small town lies directly on the slope of the Douro valley, on the
N220. There are two roads from the town worth exploring: for the first
route, leave Freixo southwards on the N220 and turn right after about
1km and then left at the next two crossroads until you reach the top of
a huge rock called Penedo Durão. Apart from affording excellent views,
this is a good place for Griffon and Egyptian Vultures, Golden Eagle,
Alpine Swift, Crag Martin, Red-rumped Swallow and Chough.

Another possibility is to leave Freixo southwards and keep on the
N220. Pass along a a very winding road that gets ever closer to the
valley and crosses the river at Barca d'Alva. An impressive line of cliffs
can be seen on your right hand side and it is worth stopping here,
looking for soaring vultures and eagles or even Peregrines. Azure-
winged Magpies are not difficult to find here; close to the river valley,
there are also Bee-eaters, Crag Martins and Golden Orioles, while the
craggy tops hold Black Wheatears.

After crossing the river in Barca d'Alva, the road leads southwards,
away from the river valley. Just a few km ahead, an isolated nest of
White Stork appears on the right side, holding the northernmost colony
of Spanish Sparrows in Portugal. After a few more km southwards, you
reach Figueira de Castelo Rodrigo, a convenient town from where to
reach the Barragem de Santa Maria de Aguiar (a reservoir). There are two
curious nests of White Stork built on dead trees just 1m over the water
line (also with many nests of Spanish Sparrows). There are also some
reed beds here, which hold Great Reed Warbler and Little Bittern. Winter
is good for wildfowl and rarities have included Great White Egret.

## 4  Ria de Aveiro

This is a large lagoon-like coastal formation located near Aveiro, in
the Beira Litoral region. The name 'Ria', used over many years,
describes the coastal development of a delta-like formation, unlike the
'rias' of different geological origin found further north in Europe. Some
authors describe these modified deltas as haff-deltas, something
particularly accurate where Aveiro's labyrinthine bay is concerned.

Formerly one of the most important estuarine wetlands in Portugal, the Ria de Aveiro has lost much of its value, due to a growing human population, heavy industrial pollution, abandoning of salt works and their conversion into fish-ponds. Illegal hunting and legal over-hunting have also affected the area. Nevertheless, it still holds the best selection of waterbirds in northern Portugal, including most of the species one would expect to find in coastal wetlands in south-western Europe. Moreover, it holds a selection of interesting land birds typical of southern Europe.

*Location*

The city of Aveiro lies 75km south of Oporto and 240km north of Lisbon, on the west coast of Portugal. It can easily be reached by taking the A1 motorway as far as Sobreiro junction and then the IP5 which runs around Aveiro. The Ria itself lies to the north and west of the town. Full details of the area can be found on the following maps: 1:100,000: 13 and 16; 1:50,000: 13-C and 16-A; 1:25,000: 163, 173, 174, 184 and 185.

*Description*

Aveiro's large wetland area is about 45km long and 12km wide, covering about 11,000ha, of which 6,000ha are non-tidal and over 1,000ha are saltpans. The water depth varies due to dredging and is generally low, apart from in the main channels or 'cales'. The intertidal vegetation is varied and ecologically quite interesting and important.

The salt-extraction industry has been much reduced, and this has lead to increasing saltpan desertion and to consequent decay of the banks and tanks. The remaining complexes have bare, grassy or bushy hummocks, tamarisk lines and some reedy ditches. Sand and mudflats are also extensive, the latter often rich in algae.

The lowland between rivers Vouga and Antuã consists of an 'enclosures' landscape. This changes gradually as one proceeds through the area to the north-west from small meadows and pastures, surrounded by tall hedges, to more open and wet ground with ditches, reedbeds, rushes, tamarisk and rice fields. In the northern sandbar, there are Maritime Pine and Acacia woods that were planted by the Forestry Service between 1888 and 1924 to conserve the dunes system. Part of this woodland and dunes is designated as a Nature Reserve; it lies between São Jacinto and the Orbitur camping site. Proliferation of alien Acacia has recently been stopped in the primary dunes and elsewhere by removing it and planting native dune grass.

The sand dunes are extensive and well-preserved along the northern sandbar. There are also large artificial sand 'dunes', resulting mainly from dredged sand deposits, like those at the end of Ilha da Mó do Meio. These, combined with the remaining dry reeds and wetter reedbeds, form a rather new but bird-rich habitat.

*Birds*

The Ria de Aveiro is good for birds at any time of year. However, like most Portuguese wetlands, it is more exciting during migration periods, particularly in autumn, when a wide variety of migrants pass through the Ria area. Species include Squacco Heron, Greater Flamingo, Montagu's Harrier, Hobby, Little Gull, Gull-billed Tern and Bonelli's Warbler. Red-rumped Swallow and Black-eared Wheatear breed away from the coast and occur here at migration time only. Shearwaters and gulls do not breed here either and, though present all year in small numbers inshore, they are much more common outside the breeding season.

In spring and early summer, breeding species like Purple Heron, Black Kite, Marsh Harrier, Black-winged Stilt, Pallid Swift, Cetti's, Great Reed and Melodious Warblers and Crested Tit all occur. These species are widespread and difficult to miss. Other interesting species which can be harder to find but are still regular here, include Little Bittern, Goshawk, Short-toed and Crested Larks, Woodlark, Savi's Warbler and Cirl Bunting.

Winter can also prove interesting, with Avocet, Crag Martin, Water Pipit, Firecrest and Bluethroat all widespread and easy to detect, while Spoonbill, Red-crested Pochard, Ferruginous Duck and Osprey occur occasionally.

*Accommodation*   To explore the area thoroughly, it is probably best to base oneself either at Aveiro or at São Jacinto on the northern sandbar. Aveiro has a variety of accommodation ranging from luxurious hotels to rented rooms. It also has a number of good restaurants. At São Jacinto the options are more limited but there is a choice between the Orbitur Camping Site (where 4-person bungalows are available), the Reserve dormitory (see p 142) or Muranzel lodge (a 'pousada'). There is a restaurant in front of the reserve headquarters and a grocery store at São Jacinto.

*Strategy*   **a) Salt-pans and Ilha da Mó do Meio**

Access to most saltpans (salinas) is difficult, as many of them lie on islets and can only be reached by boat. Luckily, there are three main complexes with access from land:

1) Marinhas de São Tiago and Lagoa do Paraíso. Leave the car at Rua da Pega (west of the University) and explore the area on foot. The lagoon is one of the best wintering areas for Little Egret, Avocet and Crag Martin, while Marsh Harrier and Peregrine can often be seen hunting here. In the saltpans there are breeding Kentish Plovers and Glossy Ibis has occurred. To the south-east, there are reedbeds, tamarisk and rushes with Cetti's, Great Reed and Melodious Warblers and Common Waxbill. Bluethroat and Dartford Warbler winter here. The mudflats can also be interesting at low tide.

2) Marinhas das Pirâmides. Follow the main city channel (Canal das Pirâmides) north-west on the left bank, passing below the IP5, until the saltpans become visible on the left side. Explore this area thoroughly, as this is usually the best place for small waders, Ruff, Little Gull, marsh terns, and Yellow Wagtail (Iberian race).

3) Marinhas da Lota. Follow the right bank of the main city channel which runs through the city from Rossio, passing under the IP5. Proceed to the fishing harbour and then turn right for the saltpans. These are very good for small waders and Black-winged Stilts. Raptors are often present, with Marsh Harrier, Black Kite and Peregrine being regularly seen. The bushy hummocks hold Dartford Warbler and sometimes Southern Grey Shrike. Bluethroats and Water Pipits occur in winter.

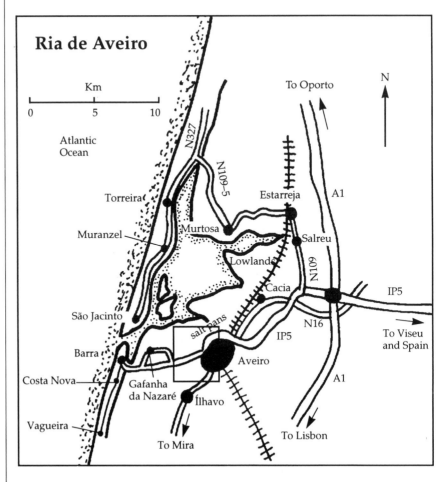

## Ria de Aveiro

Km

0     5     10

Atlantic
Ocean

N

To Oporto

N327

N109–5

A1

Torreira

Muranzel

Murtosa

Estarreja

Salreu

Lowland

N109

São Jacinto

salt pans

Cacia

IP5

N16

IP5

To Viseu
and Spain

Barra

Costa Nova

Gafanha
da Nazaré

Aveiro

Ilhavo

A1

Vagueira

To Mira

To Lisbon

1 Lagoa do Paraiso
  (mudflats)
2 Saltpans
3 Fishponds
4 Saltpans –
  Marinhas da Lota
5 Saltpans –
  Marinhas da
  Pirámides
6 University

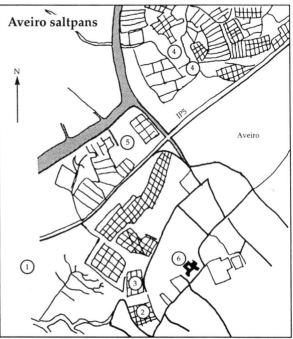

## Aveiro saltpans

N

IP5

Aveiro

4

4

5

1

3

2

6

At low tide it is worth checking Ria da Costa Nova sand-flats using the N109-7 as far as Vagueira or turning left to Gafanha do Carmo. This area holds gulls, terns and large waders such as plovers and godwits.

Ilha da Mó do Meio can easily be reached from Aveiro following the N109-7 and turning right to Gafanha da Nazaré. Continue along the road parallel to the channel as far as the Sacor Deposits, turn left and park the car near the pond, exploring the areas north and south of the road.

Breeding birds include Little Bittern, Marsh Harrier, Black Kite, Black-winged Stilt, Pallid Swift, Cetti's, Great Reed and Melodious Warblers, while in winter there are Bluethroats and Penduline Tits.

Return to the car and proceed, turning right to reach the margin of the São Jacinto channel. Check both the channel and the dunes to the east, and watch for Kentish Plover, Crested Lark and Short-toed Lark in summer.

### b) The lowlands

The lowlands between the rivers Vouga and Antuã are extensive with many bird-rich sites, only the most interesting and accessible of which are outlined here. One of the best places is at Salreu. From Aveiro, follow the IP5 as far as Cacia and then turn onto the N109 to Salreu. At Salreu turn left, cross the railway line and then proceed westwards as far as the track allows. Park the car and walk in the same direction until you reach the River Antuã (if possible, take a different track on your way back to the car). Marsh Harriers and Purple Herons are common in the larger reedbeds, which are also the best areas for Little Bittern and Savi's Warbler. Great Reed Warblers seem to prefer reedy ditches, whereas Melodious Warbler and Great Spotted Cuckoo can be found mainly on the larger hedges. White Stork and Black Kite are common as breeding species, while in autumn Squacco Heron, Red Kite, Hobby and Red-rumped Swallow occur. Spoonbill is seen on passage and may overwinter.

Another excellent area is Vilarinho/Sabadão, about 2km north-west of Cacia. Access is from Cacia to Sarrazola and Vilarinho. At Vilarinho, turn right, passing a chapel and then down to the small 'Vilarinho marsh'. Alternatively, proceed through Vilarinho, turn right to the river Vouga and then left (thus avoiding the bridge), and then follow a straight track bordered by Eucalyptus trees that runs along its left margin, passing a track through the extensive rushes where Marsh Harriers roost and Bluethroats can be seen in winter. Returning to the bridge, cross it, turn right and then proceed straight on. By this means you can explore the area to the north and return to Sarrazola by another bridge that lies further east. Common species in both areas include Hoopoe, Cetti's Warbler, Common Waxbill and Cirl Bunting, while less common birds include Little Egret, Black-winged Stilt, Crested Lark, Water Pipit, Firecrest, and Golden Oriole.

### c) Northern sandbar

Access to the northern sandbar is best from Aveiro, either by bus (from Rua Clube Galitos or from the railway station) to Forte da Barra and then by boat to S. Jacinto or by car all the way around the 'ria' through Estarreja, Veiros, Monte and Pardelhas until the N327 is reached on the sandbar. This road offers a unique view over S. Jacinto channel and the adjoining islets which lie to the east (particularly between Muranzel and S. Jacinto). There are good mudflats at low tide and some open water which is always worth checking; this is a good site for White Stork, Little Egret, Spoonbill, Greater Flamingo, Marsh Harrier and Osprey.

At the Reserva Natural das Dunas de São Jacinto there are two artificial reedy ponds and a lake (with hides and a duck trap) that hold good numbers of wintering waterfowl, particularly Wigeon, Teal, Shoveler, Pintail and occasionally Red-crested Pochard. Goshawk and Sparrowhawk are also regular here. Large number of nest boxes are spread throughout the wood and are mainly used by Coal and Great Tits. The 'Fire watch-tower' nearby is also useful for raptor watching. The Reserve Headquarters lie directly beside the N327, near its southern end, and can provide useful information to visitors.

# 5 International Tagus and the Idanha-a-Nova Plain

Southeast of Castelo Branco, the River Tagus forms a natural border between Portugal and Spain for about 40km, hence the word International, and is an excellent site for large soaring birds, such as eagles, vultures and storks. The plains around Idanha-a-Nova hold populations of bustards, sandgrouse and other steppe birds. The whole region is isolated and relatively unspoilt, offering the birdwatcher a chance to see some of the rarest and most threatened species of the Portuguese avifauna.

*Location*

This site lies approximately mid-way down Portugal's eastern border with Spain, to the east and south of the town of Castelo Branco. Full details of the area can be found on the following maps: 1:100,000: 25 and 29; 1:50,000: 25-A, 25-C and 29-A; 1:25,000: 281, 282, 283, 293, 294, 295, 304, 305, 306, 306A, 315, 315A, and 315B.

*Description*

The site stretches from the point where the River Erges joins the Tagus in the east, to the Cedillo dam, downstream to the west. The soil is schistose, which lends itself to numerous natural unvegetated rocky bluffs along the banks. These bluffs are not very high, and various rock-nesting birds breed here. The river banks and those of its tributaries, are largely covered with thick bushes of a Mediterranean garrigue type, where sun rose species dominate. The area on both sides of the river is covered in vast expanses of Cork and Holm Oak and Eucalyptus, as well as large open fields, some of which are cultivated. To the north of the river, the plain of Idanha-a-Nova, south on the town of that name, is an open, cultivated area, dotted with some rocky outcrops.

*Birds*

The International Tagus holds one of the best selections of breeding birds in mainland Portugal. Above all, it is very important for birds of prey and vultures. Resident species include Griffon and Black Vultures, Bonelli's and Golden Eagles, Red Kite, Black-shouldered Kite and Eagle

Black Stork

Owl. Summer visitors include Egyptian Vulture, Black Kite, Booted and Short-toed Eagles, Montagu's Harrier and Scops Owl, while Merlin has been seen in winter. The river valley is also important for other species such as Black Stork, Crag Martin, Red-rumped Swallow, Black Wheatear, Blue Rock Thrush and Golden Oriole.

The surrounding open areas are noted for their steppe birds, including Great and Little Bustards, Stone-curlew and Black-bellied Sandgrouse. Pin-tailed Sandgrouse has been seen here and is known to occur on the Spanish side of the Tagus. Other species include Calandra, Thekla and Short-toed Larks and Black-eared Wheatear. In the woods, which consist mainly of oak, Azure-winged Magpies and Woodchat Shrikes are abundant, and Red-necked Nightjar, Hoopoe, Orphean Warbler, Rock Sparrow and Hawfinch can also be found.

This is undoubtedly one of the best areas in Portugal for Spanish Sparrow, which is abundant, both in the villages and in the woods, and can outnumber House Sparrows in some places. Other breeding birds include Great Spotted Cuckoo, Bee-eater, Alpine Swift and Melodious Warbler.

*Accommodation*

Castelo Branco is a major town, about 40km to the west, and has a wide variety of accommodation available. Accommodation can also be found in Idanha-a-Nova, or in Monfortinho. The latter, a tourist resort, has a very good hotel and is famed for its thermal springs. Alternatively, it is possible to camp in the wild or to ask for Quercus, an environmentalist organisation that has some basic accommodation near Rosmaninhal (booking in advance is advisable, tel. 077-47196).

At Rosmaninhal, there is a small café where lunch can be arranged, if ordered a few hours in advance. There is also a restaurant at Zebreira.

*Strategy*

This is a vast area, and a car is essential to explore it thoroughly. Spring is by far the most rewarding birding season, because the variety of species is greater and the weather is usually pleasant. In midsummer, the temperature can exceed 40°C making it dangerously hot at midday. A day is enough to see most birds, though the beauty and richness of

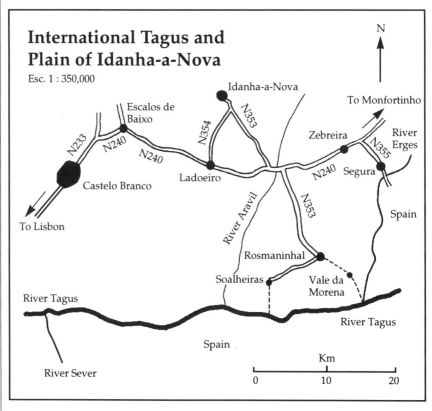

**International Tagus and Plain of Idanha-a-Nova**

Esc. 1 : 350,000

the area make it worth a stay of several days, time permitting.

From Castelo Branco, follow the N233 for 5km and then fork right onto the N240 eastwards to Ladoeiro. A stop at this village may be worth while as Spanish Sparrows are plentiful here. Nests may also be noted on telegraph poles and in trees along the road.

The Idanha-a-Nova plain can be explored by following road N354 northbound from Ladoeiro or the N353, which runs north from slightly further east. The plain is a good site for steppe birds, such as Little Bustard and Stone-curlew, and there is even a small population of Great Bustard present, while Black-shouldered Kites can be seen at dusk and dawn.

The N353 leads from Idanha-a-Nova southeastwards and meets the N240 near Ribeira do Aravil (the Aravil River). Along the river there are Bee-eater, Red-rumped Swallow and Melodious Warbler. The fields around the cross-roads have Thekla and Short-toed Larks, as well as Black-bellied Sandgrouse. There is also a chance of seeing Egyptian Vulture and Great Spotted Cuckoo here.

From here, follow the N353 south to Rosmaninhal, from where an unsurfaced road leads south-east to a farm called Vale da Morena (a detailed map, no. 306, is useful and permission needs to be obtained at the farm to proceed to the river). The area consists mainly of open fields and Holm Oaks and holds a variety of breeding birds, including Montagu's Harrier, Red-necked Nightjar, Short-toed and Calandra Larks, Black-eared Wheatear, Orphean Warbler, Raven and Rock Sparrow.

The river valley is the best place for soaring Black Storks, vultures, large eagles, and kites and near the mouth of the River Erges, Black Wheatear, Blue Rock Thrush, Crag Martin and Orphean Warbler can also be found, while Golden Orioles can be heard singing and occasionally fly across the valley. There are more colonies of Spanish Sparrows in the nearby woods.

Further east, past Zebreira, the N355 crosses the border at Segura. The bridge over the River Erges here is a good stopping point to locate Black Stork, Egyptian Vulture and Alpine Swift.

# 6 Boquilobo Marsh

Boquilobo Marsh is one of the most important inland wetlands in Portugal. It is famous for its breeding and wintering waterbirds and particularly for its heronry. However, the area is farmed intensively and pollution is a problem.

*Location*

Boquilobo Marsh is located about 100km north-east of Lisbon, quite close to the little town of Golegã, not far from the Tagus River. Full details of the area can be found on the following maps: 1:100,000: 27; 1:50,000: 27-C; 1:25,000: 329 and 341.

*Description*

This small but attractive wetland area is a nature reserve, with some restrictions on human access. It is fed by the River Almonda, which inundates the surrounding fields. However, a proportion of these are drained in early summer, so that some sites are not always under water.

This area is interesting both to the ornithologist and to the botanist. There are large areas of willow, especially alongside the river, and much aquatic vegetation. The surrounding areas are mainly agricultural. There are a few wood groves, consisting mainly of Cork Oaks, but some of these have been felled in recent years.

*Birds*

During the breeding season, it is possible to see a wide variety of herons, most of which breed in the heronry: Cattle Egrets, Little Egrets and Night Herons are all common. In recent years, a few Spoonbills – about 10 pairs – have been breeding here as well. Squacco Heron is much rarer and, although breeding is not confirmed every year, there are usually two or three birds present. In the wetter areas of aquatic vegetation, one can watch Purple Herons and Little Bitterns side by side.

Other breeding waterbirds include Whiskered Tern, but numbers are highly variable, depending to some degree on climatic conditions. In good years, there can be up to 120 breeding pairs. Water Rails are resident but, as usual, are very secretive. Baillon's Crake has been observed here and there is suitable breeding habitat for the species. Red-crested Pochard has bred.

Birds of prey have decreased due to habitat destruction in the surrounding areas. Black Kite occurs in summer, while Booted and Short-toed Eagles are regularly seen. Marsh Harrier and Hobby can be seen on passage.

Among the breeding passerines, the most interesting species are to be found in the areas of aquatic vegetation: Cetti's, Reed and Great Reed Warblers are all widespread and common, together with introduced Common Waxbills. Savi's Warbler is much scarcer and hard to find, though its song may betray its presence long before one locates it by eye. The surrounding areas hold Bee-eater, Melodious Warbler, Woodchat Shrike, Golden Oriole and Rock Sparrow.

In winter, large numbers of ducks congregate here. Shoveler and Teal are the most numerous species, but Pintail is also quite numerous and, in some years, the marsh holds about 1% of the European wintering population. Ospreys winter regularly in the area. Smaller birds to be found in winter include Redwing, Penduline Tit, Brambling, and Siskin, most of them widespread.

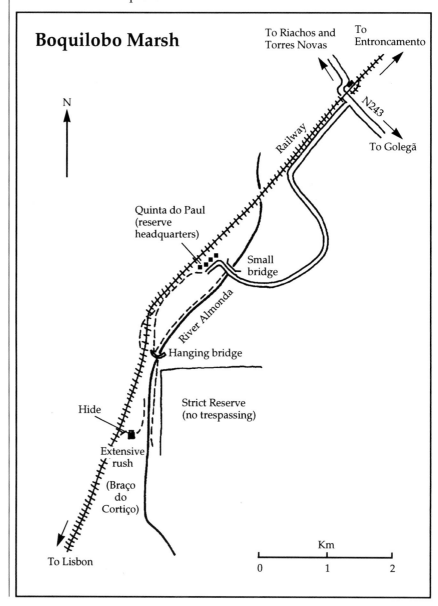

It is possible to stay at Golegã, either at the camp site or at a pension. Alternatively, it is possible to find accommodation at Torres Novas, Santarém or Entroncamento.

Spring is undoubtedly the best time of year to visit the marsh, although it can be interesting throughout the year.

If travelling by car from Lisbon, it is advisable to take the A1 and leave it after 95km, following the signs for Torres Novas. This is the IP6, but you have to leave it after about 10km and enquire for the road to Riachos. This village is reached a few kilometres further on and after passing through the village and over the railway line, take a surfaced road to the right and follow it until you reach a small bridge over the river Almonda. The reserve headquarters lies about 200 metres ahead.

Although quite small in size, Boquilobo Marsh is not very easy to explore. The whole area is a nature reserve, and the most central area is a controlled reserve, with human access severely restricted. A large part of the marsh is covered by water throughout the year, but the water level is very variable and in wet years, when rain fall is plentiful, the main paths can occasionally be under water, making it impossible to walk into the marsh. Rainfall here varies over a range of 500mm and it is virtually impossible to predict water levels. Access to the best areas is rather difficult.

Park near the headquarters and return to the bridge over the River Almonda. From here a path runs parallel to the river on the north-west side and can be walked easily. It is lined with poplars and willows and offers views over the marsh and its birds. There is another marked nature trail which leads from the park headquarters and from which one can watch Whiskered Terns and feeding egrets. After a 30-minute walk, there is a hanging cable bridge (dangerous!), which can be used to cross the river to watch the breeding herons and Whiskered Terns. However, this lies at the edge of a strict reserve and it is forbidden to walk any further.

Proceeding further south along the west side of the river, one reaches a pool (Braço do Cortiço) covered with dense rushes, with a small hide on its northern shore. This is one of the best sites for Purple Heron and Little Bittern. Other birds here include Water Rail and Great Reed and Savi's Warblers.

This site is also quite convenient for those without a car, as it can easily be reached by train. From Lisbon, there are hourly departures to Entroncamento; leave the train at Mato de Miranda, which is reached in about 1 hour and 25 minutes. Walk parallel to the railway line from the station, following one of the nearby trails for about 2.5km, watching for small woodland birds, including Woodlark, Sardinian Warbler, Short-toed Treecreeper, Serin and Rock Sparrow. Near km 96 there is a small 'bridge' on the railway line, which lies close to the hide of the 'Braço do Cortiço', as described above.

# 7 Tagus Estuary

The Tagus River is 960km long and runs from the Sierra de Guadarrama in Spain through central Portugal, reaching the sea at

Lisbon, where it forms a very wide estuary. This is the most important wetland area in Portugal and one of the most important in Europe. Its bird life is extraordinarily rich, and over 240 species have been recorded. Its waterbird populations are particularly significant. In a relatively small area, it concentrates large numbers of southern European birds, among them some of the most interesting and rare species.

*Location*

The estuary lies to the east of Lisbon, the capital city of Portugal, which is located two-thirds of the way down Portugal's west coast. Full details of the area can be found on the following maps: 1:100,000: 34; 1:50,000: 34-B and 34-D; 1:25,000: 404, 418, and 432.

*Description*

Like many estuaries, it is surrounded by densely populated and industrialised areas. Lisbon and its surroundings together contain almost two million inhabitants, most of them living close to the river. However, the eastern part of the estuary, from Porto Alto to Alcochete, is less densely populated and has been declared a nature reserve covering about 14,000ha.

The reserve covers much of the intertidal mudflats, where most waterbirds feed. There are also vast areas of saltmarsh, large reedbeds and hundreds of saltpans, some of which are abandoned and are currently being altered for use as fish ponds. There are several man-made dykes along the river, which protect the surrounding plains from flood damage in wet years and from the effects of spring tides, which in winter are often augmented by strong onshore westerly winds. The plains here consist mainly of arable land, dry pastures and rice fields and are criss-crossed by a dense network of drainage canals. The banks of these canals are often heavily vegetated with a mixture of fresh water and halophytic vegetation.

Further inland, there are scattered wooded areas, where Cork Oak predominates. There are also some Pine and Eucalyptus plantations and, close to water bodies, Poplars, Willows and densely vegetated ditches. Filled with a tangle of briars and rather moist even in summer, these are attractive not only to birds but also to butterflies, moths and small vertebrates.

*Birds*

Given its geographical location and its ecological diversity, the area is important for both migrating and wintering waterbird populations. Outside the breeding season, mainly from late July through to early May, the mudflats are alive with waders. At high tide, the flocks swarm across the sky, gyrating and jinking in the wake of raptors, as they fly to the non-tidal saltpans and inland fields.

Waders are very numerous in the area. The wintering population of Avocets is particularly noteworthy; over 50% (c.12,000) of Europe's winter population can be seen here, sometimes in one vast snowstorm of swirling birds. Other waders that winter in very large numbers include Dunlin, Redshank, Grey, Ringed and Kentish Plovers and Black-tailed Godwits. Most other European species of wader occur regularly on passage, often in considerable numbers: these include

Mediterranean Gull

Curlew Sandpiper, Little Stint, Knot, Whimbrel, Bar-tailed Godwit, Greenshank, Spotted Redshank and Snipe. Other less common species, such as Temminck's Stint, are regularly recorded.

Wintering wildfowl are numerous, the most common species being Teal, Mallard, Wigeon, Shoveler and Greylag Goose, while Garganey and Pintail are less numerous and occur mainly on passage.

Depending upon the season, gulls and terns may be very common, forming large flocks. In late summer and autumn, it is possible to find interesting species, such as Mediterranean Gull and Gull-billed and Black Terns; rarities have included Ring-billed Gull and White-winged Black Tern.

Other interesting wintering species include Water Pipit, Bluethroat and Penduline Tit.

During the breeding season, most waterbirds are absent. However, it is possible to find an interesting suite of species, many of which are typical of southern Europe. Breeding species include Purple Heron, White Stork, Collared Pratincole, Black-winged Stilt, Kentish Plover, Little Tern, Hoopoe, Bee-eater, Common and Pallid Swifts, Wood, Crested and Short-toed Larks, Yellow Wagtail (Iberian race), various warblers (including Reed, Great Reed, Cetti's and Sardinian), Southern Grey and Woodchat Shrikes, Spotless Starling, Azure-winged Magpie, Rock Sparrow, Common Waxbill and Serin. Less common birds include Little Bittern, Stone-curlew, Whiskered Tern, Red-necked and European Nightjars, Calandra Lark, Tawny Pipit, Savi's and Melodious Warblers, Golden Oriole, and Hawfinch.

This site is a good area for birds of prey. In summer Black Kite, Black-

shouldered Kite, Booted Eagle, Short-toed Eagle, Marsh Harrier and
Montagu's Harrier are present. Outside the breeding season Osprey,
Hen Harrier, Merlin and Peregrine occur.

Cattle and Little Egrets do not breed in the area, but are usually
widespread outside the breeding season, either feeding or roosting.
Greater Flamingos can be seen in good numbers throughout the year
and have been increasing in numbers over the past few years, with up
to 2,000 birds counted in late summer.

On autumn passage (mainly August to October), migrants species
include: Great Spotted Cuckoo (until mid August), Alpine Swift, Roller,
Redstart, Whinchat, Wheatear, Whitethroat, Sedge, Subalpine and
Grasshopper Warblers, and Pied and Spotted Flycatchers. Ortolan
Buntings can occasionally be found in the stubble fields.

*Accommodation*

The area lies some 45 minutes from Lisbon, which is by far the most
convenient centre for exploration and where accommodation facilities
are numerous and varied. It is also possible to stay at Alcochete,
Montijo, Porto Alto and Vila Franca de Xira. There are good restaurants
at Porto Alto.

*Strategy*

For those staying in Lisbon, the best way to leave the city is
northwards on the A1 towards Oporto, veering right at km 24 (where
signposts read Vila Franca de Xira, Elvas and Évora). Passing through
the toll gate, veer left slightly following signs for Vila Franca and after a
few hundred metres, signs will indicate Porto Alto. Follow these until
you are crossing the metal bridge over the Tagus. The road here is the
N10, which runs eastwards to Porto Alto junction, a reference point
used throughout this site description.

Due to the richness of the area, this site description has been divided
into four different subsections. It is not an exaggeration to suggest that
two or three days in the area are necessary to cover all the habitats.

**a)  Ponta da Erva plains**

This is a clearly delimited flat area, lying between the River Tagus
and its smaller tributary, the Sorraia river. The northern boundary is the
N10. At the southern point of these 'plains', called Ponta da Erva, the
two rivers meet. The whole of the area is rather featureless, with few
trees and very few houses. Most of the land is ploughed and cultivated,
or left as dry pasture, though intensive rice cultivation grows apace.
The plains are surrounded by a dyke, which prevents winter flooding
and are criss-crossed by many ditches, all looking rather similar.

To reach the area, turn right about 300m after crossing the Vila Franca
de Xira bridge and take the wide, unsurfaced track that leads
southwards through the fields (passable throughout the year). When
driving between the fields on the ubiquitous dirt tracks, it is advisable
to stop frequently and scan for birds. During the breeding season, you
can find Montagu's Harrier, Collared Pratincole, Short-toed and
Calandra Larks. In winter, the fields hold Lapwing, Golden Plover,
Marsh and Hen Harriers, Little Bustard and the occasional Merlin.

After about 9km, the road forks (point A on the map). To the south

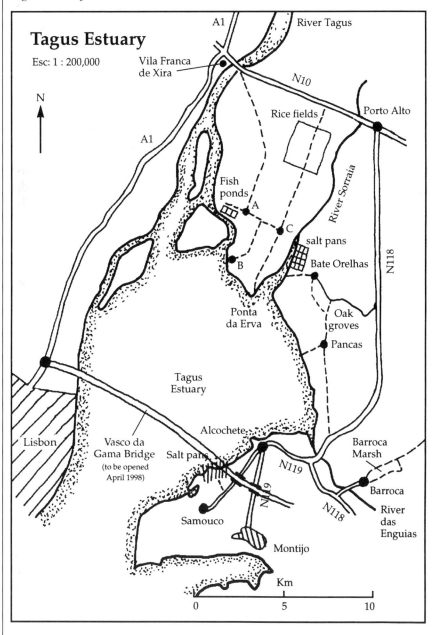

(500m), there are three fish ponds; they can hold interesting waders, ducks and, sometimes, Greater Flamingos, as well as Bluethroats in winter. Proceeding eastwards from point A, take the first track to the right after about 700m, near a farm entrance. This ends after about 2km, close to the main dyke (point B on the map). The track may be blocked by a wire gate – if so walk from here; beware bulls. Walk along the dyke, either to the right or to the left. In summer, Purple Herons, Marsh Harriers, Yellow Wagtail, and Savi's and Great Reed Warblers are present. The vegetation along the dyke is good for migrating warblers and flycatchers in late summer and autumn, and for Cetti's and Sardinian Warblers throughout the year, while the reedbeds hold wintering Bluethroats and Penduline Tits. In winter geese, ducks, waders and Greater Flamingos can be seen from the dyke and Ospreys sometimes roost nearby.

Proceeding eastwards from Point A but not turning right to point B, continue ahead until the road ends at a T-junction, which is point C on the map. From here, take the road that runs southwards to Ponta da Erva, where Greater Flamingos and wildfowl can be seen, along with waders and terns.

Return to point C, drive 5km northwards and just before the main road stop at the extensive rice fields to look for Purple Heron, Black-winged Stilt, Whiskered Tern and Collared Pratincole.

### b) Pancas

This area lies on the east bank of the river Sorraia. Its landscape differs significantly from that of Ponta da Erva, with many wooded groves of pine and Cork Oak.

From Porto Alto (see above), take the N118, to the south, following the signs to Alcochete, and turn right after 10km, where a small signpost reads Pancas (at km 21.5). Follow the tarmac road for 500m, stop at the first curve, where sand is being excavated, and park well off the road. The surrounding woodland is a good spot for European Nightjar after dusk, as well as for Bee-eater, Cetti's and Melodious Warblers, Iberian Chiffchaff and Cirl Bunting. The road can then be followed until a small collection of farm buildings (called Bate-Orelhas) is reached. Proceed straight onwards for about 250m on an unsurfaced sand track, until a green gate is reached. Even if the gate is open, you should leave the car outside and walk the track. Here raptors use the thermals over the sandy fields in summer. This is a long, hot haul in summer but is an excellent area for Black-shouldered Kite, and the saltpans at the end of this track are one of the major sites for rare waders, gulls and terns. The list of rarer species seen at the saltpans includes Pectoral Sandpiper and Wilson's Phalarope. It is advisable to check the tides before exploring this area, for at low tide the saltpans may be completely empty.

From Bate-Orelhas, it is also possible to follow another unsurfaced track to the south that leads through a Cork Oak grove to look for Azure-winged Magpie, Short-toed Treecreeper, Woodchat Shrike and Rock Sparrow, or for soaring raptors. At dusk, this area is good for both nightjars. The track ends at a 'T'-junction, the left fork returning to the main road and the right one leading to another farm on a slight elevation called Pancas. On reaching Pancas farm, veer left and continue through vineyards and then through mixed Cork Oak and eucalyptus groves. The view over the estuary is excellent at this point and flocks of distant Greater Flamingos can often be seen. Black-shouldered Kites are frequently found hunting here, especially towards evening.

### c) Barroca Marsh and Rilvas

The Barroca Marsh (Paul da Barroca), which lies to the south-east of Alcochete, consists mainly of rice fields. Leave Porto Alto as above (see under Pancas), and turn left after about 20km on to the N118, where signposts read Setúbal and Montijo. After 3km, there is a road to the left, signposted Barroca d'Alva, and the village of Barroca is reached after 1.5km. It is possible to cross through the village and follow one of the unsurfaced tracks – the left one runs through rice fields, while the right one passes through Cork Oak woods. The ditches and the small pools here are covered with dense vegetation and hold several interesting species. Breeding birds include Little Bittern, Purple Heron and Great Reed Warbler, as well as three introduced species – Yellow-crowned Bishop, Red Avadavat and Village Weaver. Large flocks of Black-tailed Godwit feed in this area in winter. The surrounding woods hold birds of prey, while many of the electricity poles are topped with the nests of White Storks.

### d) Alcochete

The area around Alcochete consists mainly of the exposed river banks of the Tagus and saltpans and is a good site for close views of Greater Flamingos.

Alcochete can be reached from Porto Alto, by following the N118, to the south, or from Lisbon, by crossing the river on the enormous 25th April Bridge, taking the A2 motorway and leaving it after 18km, following the signs to Barreiro, then to Montijo and finally to Alcochete (a new bridge will connect Lisbon directly to Montijo; it will be opened in 1998). From Alcochete, follow the N119, to the east for about 2km, and turn left immediately before the BP petrol station, following the road to Hortas (c.900m) to the river bank. Leave the car and explore the surrounding mudflats, as this is one of the best watching points for wildfowl and waders at high or low tide.

This area can also be reached from Lisbon by using the public transport network. From Praça do Comércio, there are hourly boats to Montijo, from where a bus can be taken to Alcochete. Leave the bus at Alcochete to explore the shore from here.

## 8 Lisbon and the Estoril Coast

Despite being built up, the city and the coast around Lisbon offer the birdwatcher with no more than a few hours to spend some interesting surprises. Although not one of the more famed birdwatching sites in the country, over 130 species have been recorded within the city limits so far. Interesting habitats in the area include city parks, the river shore and two capes, one for migrants and one with good sea-watching potential.

*Location*

Lisbon is the capital city of Portugal and is located two-thirds of the way down Portugal's west coast. Full details of the area can be found on the following maps: 1:100,000: 34; 1:50,000: 34-A, 34-C and 34-D; 1:25,000: 415, 429, 430 and 431.

*Description*

Lisbon lies on the northern bank of the Tagus estuary, which stretches west reaching the open sea at Cascais. What were once small fishing hamlets and beach-side villages such as Algés, Carcavelos and

Estoril are now incorporated into an unbroken strip of development, which grows ever westwards and northwards. The hinterland is a mixture of small villages, with cultivated fields, scrubland, factories and rubble, all backed by the Sintra hills. The western tip of the east-west Sintra axis runs into the sea at Cape da Roca, the westernmost point in continental Europe.

Near Lisbon's centre, between Praça do Comércio and Rossio, it is possible to find the oldest buildings (most are post-1755). The further one gets away from the older historic part of the city, the more recent and ugly become the buildings. However, around the edge of this ever-expanding metropolis, the density of buildings decreases and there are several small to medium-sized parks, and open and wooded areas.

In the western half of the city, Monsanto Park forms the only really large green area. It is transected nowadays by a dense road network, traffic is usually heavy and it is not advisable to wander too far into the park with expensive optics on show. However, the Tapada da Ajuda, which lies on the southern part of the park is surrounded by a 2m wall, and is relatively free of traffic. It is an interesting area, consisting of wooded and semi-open habitats.

There is an artificial sea-wall, which extends from Algés to Moscavide. Near Praça do Comércio, close to the city centre, there is a ferry boat terminal.

West of Lisbon, the bank of the River Tagus also provides a variety of habitats. From Cascais, in the west, through Carcavelos to Algés, the coast line alternates between beaches and rocky sectors. North and west of Cascais lie two headlands, Cape Raso and Cape da Roca. The hinterland consists of pine wood, allotments and built up areas.

*Birds*

During migration times (April-May and August to October), passage can be heavy and continuous with some of the summer visitors typical of Spain and Portugal clearly evident.

Common breeding species in Lisbon include Swift, Pallid Swift, Black Redstart, Fan-tailed Warbler, Sardinian Warbler, Short-toed Treecreeper, and Serin, while Firecrest and Spotless Starling are present but harder to find. In early autumn, migrants occurring on passage include chats, warblers and flycatchers. Interesting species which have occurred within the city limits include White and Black Storks, Booted Eagle, Black Kite, Peregrine, Alpine Swift, Subalpine Warbler, Woodchat Shrike, Golden Oriole and Hawfinch. Crossbills pass south over Lisbon in irruption years.

However, it is the littoral and deep water birds that make the area worth exploring. From August onwards the beaches form overnight roosts for gulls and terns, and sometimes waders, and the sewage outlets at Cruz Quebrada, Caxias, Oeiras and Carcavelos can be excellent for marsh terns, especially when the winds blow from the east. Interesting waders such as Whimbrel, Turnstone, Sanderling and Purple Sandpiper may occur in the area outside the breeding season, on the beaches or flying over the sea during seawatches.

Lesser Black-backed Gulls are common from August to early April. Yellow-legged Gulls are resident in Portugal and occur in this area mainly to the west of Cascais. Other species of gulls occur in autumn and winter, with Mediterranean Gulls numerous after gales from the west. Onshore west-north-west winds and rain bring Cory's and Mediterranean Shearwaters close inshore and the list of seabirds seen off the Cape Raso area include Sooty Shearwater, Wilson's Storm Petrel and Sabine's and Audouin's Gulls. Great and Arctic Skuas occur almost all year round, although they are more frequent during autumn and winter.

*Accommodation*  There are hosts of pensões, hotels and aparthotels in Lisbon and in many of the villages along the coast line, such as Estoril and Cascais. Any travel agency will be happy to arrange something and even in the high season it is usually possible to obtain accommodation. Car hire, which can be arranged through hotels, travel agencies and tourist information offices, is not cheap in Portugal and it is worth planning one's route around Lisbon with care to maximise observations and minimise costs.

*Strategy*  Buy a map of Lisbon and, unless you already have a rental car, use local transport – trains, trams, buses and taxis.

In the old quarters of Bairro Alto, Chiado, Rossio and Alfama there are important colonies of Pallid Swifts, and birds can be seen from late March to late September (Common Swift is also a common breeder throughout the city, mainly in the modern parts). Black Redstarts breed

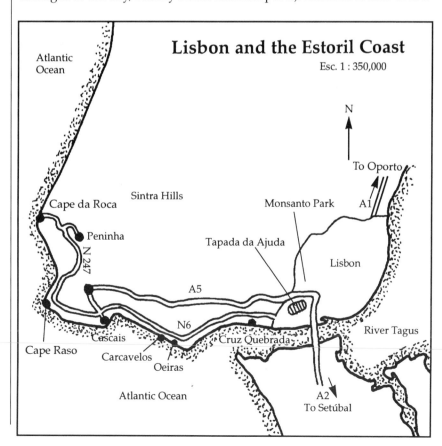

throughout most of the city, except possibly in the most modern built-up areas. The city parks have resident Blackcaps, as well as Greenfinch, Serin and, in the case of the largest ones (like Monteiro-Mor, near Lumiar), Sardinian Warbler and Short-toed Treecreeper.

In the large Monsanto Park there is too much disturbance to allow for large or diverse bird populations to become established. However, the Tapada da Ajuda holds several interesting breeding species, including Fan-tailed Warbler, Sardinian Warbler, Short-toed Treecreeper, Spotless Starling and Serin. Outside the breeding season, other species do occur, and early morning autumn migration can be heard as well as seen. The Tapada lies very close to the 25th April Bridge and is best reached from Alcântara.

It is worth looking for migrating terns in the middle of the estuary. The best ferry from which to observe terns is the boat from Lisbon to Barreiro. The terminus is at Praça do Comércio.

The coastline to the west can also be exciting. The 'Marginal' corniche hugs the coast here and it is merely a matter of motoring along to likely beach sites. Do not stop on this road or attempt to birdwatch while driving here; use the available lay-bys.

The rail line from Cascais to Lisbon passes close to the sea and the stations are clearly marked. Avoid the trains that travel non-stop to Lisbon – the trains are colour-coded in the front window and easy to identify. All the beaches are worth examining. There is a coastal walk-way between Cascais and S. Pedro do Estoril and another along the Carcavelos-Oeiras shore, which is one of the best sites for wintering Purple Sandpipers in the country. The Algés beach is also recommended for passage waders and terns, especially during easterly winds, but do not ignore the sewage outlet further west, near Cruz Quebrada station. Autumn/winter is probably the best time for examining the beaches – each small patch of sand and rock may be full of gulls and overwintering Sandwich Terns. Mediterranean Gulls winter here, along with two subspecies of Lesser Black-backed Gull. Ring-billed Gull occurs annually.

For seawatching continue through Cascais and, following the road past Boca do Inferno, stop at Cape Raso's red metal lighthouse. This lies 6km west of Cascais and is easily reached by car (follow signs for Guincho) or by bus from Cascais railway station (the bus stops outside the lighthouse). Seawatching is most productive around dawn.

Cape da Roca, which lies further north is too high for seawatching, but its valleys are excellent in autumn for passage migrants. Peregrine of the race *brookei* is regular and Eleonora's Falcon has been seen here. Systematic birdwatching here would probably reap rewards. The small palace of Peninha lies directly above Cape da Roca and is a regular winter haunt of Alpine Accentor and Snow Bunting.

# 9 Cape Espichel and Serra da Arrábida

Between the estuaries of the Tagus and the Sado lies an area of overdeveloped urban sprawl, some wonderful coastal scenery and an imposing limestone range, running east-west for 50km. The western end of the range reaches the sea at Cape Espichel, an isolated promontory with small farms and a lighthouse. This peninsula is particularly interesting at migration times, but there are also some attractive southern European species breeding here. There are three main areas worth investigating within this site: Albufeira Lagoon, Cape Espichel and Arrábida Natural Park.

*Location*

This site lies to the south of Lisbon on the west coast of Portugal. Full details of the area can be found on the following maps: 1:100,000: 38; 1:50,000: 38-B; 1:25,000: 453, 454, 464, and 465.

*Description*

This is a curious area geologically, surrounded to the north-west and south by the sea and backed by the Serra da Arrábida, which stretches along an east-west axis and is an area of superb scenery. Cape Espichel, at the western tip of the Serra, is mainly limestone karst with pockets of vegetation and some pine plantations. The soil is poor and cultivation rather desultory.

The Serra da Arrábida is not high as Iberian ranges go, but its landscape is very characteristic with limestone outcrops peeping out from a dense cover of Mediterranean scrub ('carrascais'). The vegetation is dominated by Kermes Oak, Strawberry Tree and Tree Heather. At long range the inclined strata lines of limestone lend the peaks a unique aspect.

Arrábida is one of Portugal's best known Natural Parks, with restrictions on the construction of buildings and preservation orders on some of the older buildings. However, the Serra is now under threat from two quarries, one at either end, which will irrevocably alter its shape and character.

*Birds*

Cape Espichel is very dry, with a mesoclimate compounded by its porous limestone geology. During the breeding season, the most interesting species are Pallid Swift, Bee-eater, Woodlark, Black Redstart, Blue Rock Thrush and Cirl Bunting.

It is far more interesting at migration times, basically due to its strategic location on one of Iberia's flyways. The intensity of spring migration is dependent on wind, but typically will include a small regular passage of Turtle Doves, various swifts, as well as a good selection of passerines.

The autumn passage lasts from August through October to mid November and is marked by a regular passage of trans-saharan migrants – swifts, hirundines, Whinchat, Melodious, Willow, and Subalpine Warblers, flycatchers, Woodchat Shrike, and sometimes Roller. Short-toed Larks, Tawny Pipits and Ortolan Buntings are regular. Unlike at Sagres further south, birds of prey tend not to concentrate at Espichel, but Eleonora's and Red-footed Falcons and Lesser Kestrel have all been observed and Short-toed and Booted Eagles are seen occasionally.

At Albufeira Lagoon, a little to the north of Cape Espichel, herons, ducks, coots and gulls make up the bulk of birds but careful watching has produced Bittern, Little Bittern, Brent Goose, Osprey, and Goshawk as well as excellent winter numbers of Crag Martins and sometimes other hirundines.

Arrábida is a picturesque area. Summer is marked by the presence of breeding birds such as Bonelli's Eagle, Alpine and Pallid Swifts, Red-necked Nightjar, Wood and Crested Larks, Red-rumped Swallow, Blue Rock Thrush, Iberian Chiffchaff, Woodchat Shrike, Golden Oriole, Hawfinch and Cirl Bunting. Falls of migrants passing southwards along Portugal's west coast or reaching the coast at daybreak often occur in these hills and in autumn a wide variety of trans-saharan migrants can be seen. In winter Firecrest is a regular visitor.

*Accommodation*     The whole area is accessible by car from Lisbon or Setúbal; both are cosmopolitan cities with a wealth of accommodation. Nearer to Cape Espichel, the fishing village of Sesimbra has many pensões and hotels (including four-star). The Hotel de Zimbras on the road to the cape from Santana is a good base from which to reach Cape Espichel quickly in the morning to watch passage migration.

*Strategy*     All three sites can be visited in a day trip, though Cape Espichel is definitely best in the four hours after dawn.

### a) Cape Espichel

Approaching from Lisbon, cross the Tagus by following signs indicating 'SUL PONTE'. The bridge toll is only paid on the northward journey (150 Esc. as of 1997). After about 10km leave the motorway near Fogueteiro and follow the N378, which is signposted Sesimbra. Proceed through Fernão Ferro and, at Santana, go directly through the village, until the road forks left to Sesimbra and right to Cape Espichel. Follow the right fork and continue following the signs to Cape Espichel. The village of Azóia marks the beginning of Cape Espichel proper.

The best strategy on reaching Azóia is to continue for about 1km towards the Convento de Nossa Senhora de Espichel before turning onto a rough track to the left. Leave the car here and walk through the unfenced fields along lines of pistachio bushes to the lighthouse. From late August to early October, Ortolan Buntings are very regular here, along with Subalpine Warblers and *Phylloscopus* warblers including Bonelli's Warbler. In the early autumn, Short-toed Larks, Tawny Pipits and Yellow Wagtails are regular diurnal migrants, succeeded as the autumn progresses by Skylarks, White Wagtails and finches. Dotterel and Richard's Pipit have been seen here. From the lighthouse (where the 'gardens' are worth examining), a track leads to the Convent. The track passes near an enclosed 'garden' with fig and eucalyptus which is well worth investigating for migrating flycatchers, chats, warblers, and buntings. Local resident birds include Black Redstart, Blue Rock Thrush, Rock Sparrow, and Cirl Bunting. The old crumbling walls of the Convent complex offer ready cover and should be carefully examined. The valley between the Convent and the lighthouse is scrub-covered and can be excellent in windy easterly conditions when other sites are difficult to watch.

The north side of the headland between the Convent and Azóia is

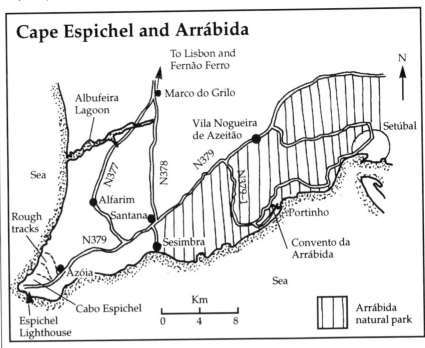

Cape Espichel and Arrábida

also worth checking and is approached via rough tracks, best travelled on foot. On reaching Azóia from Santana take the first track right behind a small café where signs indicate 'C. Velho'. Follow this track for 300m and despite appearances to the contrary, walk between the houses and immediately turn left onto a worn path just wide enough for a car. This path winds down through pines, 'gardens' and fallow crop fields. Closer to the headland is a second track again to the north, opposite a line of permanently 'half-built' holiday homes. This track is not negotiable by car but is worth walking – the habitat is ideal for a wide variety of migrants. The third track to the north is reached by turning north onto a mud track beside the old stone aqueduct. This walk is excellent for flycatchers, shrikes and buntings.

## b) Albufeira Lagoon

To reach Albufeira Lagoon from Lisbon, follow the route to Fernão Ferro and turn right at Marco do Grilo where signs indicate Lagoa de Albufeira. If coming from Cape Espichel, turn left to Alfarim. On reaching Alfarim, bear right for the lagoon. Continuing along this road returns you to Fernão Ferro. The eastern arm of the lake runs parallel to the road (N377) and though entry is prohibited, the most interesting areas can be viewed from the road along the eastern end. A telescope is an advantage here and morning viewing is best because of the light. For many years the area was prey to overdevelopment and eutrophication but timely action has saved the site and now it is possible to see large numbers of Coots, other waterfowl and a variety of passage migrants.

## c) Arrábida

Arrábida can be approached from Setúbal, although it is considerably easier to go to Santana (as described above) and at the roundabout outside the village turn through 270° until signposts read Azeitão. Continue along this road for about 10km, then turn sharply to the right at a sign reading Arrábida. The N379-1 takes you to the more exposed heights of Arrábida, where Bonelli's Eagle, Alpine and Pallid Swifts and Azure-winged Magpie can be regularly seen. In autumn, migrant passerines are plentiful.

This road, N379-1, also provides access to the south-facing slopes of Arrábida and numerous small tracks lead into the scrub – the characteristic sclerophyllous woodland dominated by Kermes Oak. Small secluded valleys of Lusitanian Oak on the seaward slopes and in particular where the road runs down to the village of Portinho da Arrábida are well worth exploring, especially in the mornings. Access to most of Arrábida is open and there are many walking tracks but certain parts are restricted. A visit to the Convento da Arrábida is worthwhile for breathtaking views and access to some of the species mentioned above.

# 10 Sado Estuary

This large wetland is currently a Nature Reserve which extends over 23,000ha. The northern shore suffers from heavy development and ugly pollution, but the rest of the area has remained relatively undeveloped, apart of course from extensive agricultural activity, centred on rice production. The whole area is biologically rich and varied, forming one of the best sites for birdwatching in Portugal. There are breeding, passage and wintering waterbirds, as well as a remarkable variety of breeding and passage passerines.

**Location**    This site lies about 50km south of Lisbon on the west coast of Portugal. Access from Lisbon is straightforward using the A2 to Setúbal. Full details of the area can be found on the following maps: 1:100,000: 39; 1:50,000: 39-A and 39-C; 1:25,000: 454, 455, 465, 466, 467, 475, and 476.

**Description**    The landscape of the estuary is varied. It is 35km long, from the mouth in the north-west of the area, near Setúbal, to Alcácer do Sal, in the south-east. The estuary is wide, but very shallow and when the tide is low, most of its surface is exposed as estuarine mud flats.

The river banks are covered in places with large areas of saltmarsh and reeds. There are extensive complexes of saltpans (salinas) all around the estuary, particularly on the northern shore, to the west of Zambujal and on the southern shore, to the west of Alcácer. Small freshwater pools, such as Murta Dam, occur throughout the area; many of these are also surrounded by large patches of reeds and willows.

The wooded areas are very important, extending as they do for many kilometres. On the northern shore, they consist mainly of dense formations of Cork Oaks, together with Maritime Pine, while on the southern shore Umbrella Pine is by far the dominant species, though other trees occur.

The peninsula of Tróia, forming the western limit of the estuary, separates it from the Atlantic. It consists almost entirely of sand, densely vegetated with bushes, such as Acacia and plantations of Maritime Pine and Eucalyptus.

The Sapal da Carrasqueira is a small treeless peninsula of land that extends into the estuary northwards of Comporta. It lies immediately to the east of the Tróia peninsula and is surrounded by a dyke, in order to prevent flooding; rice is cultivated extensively here. The extreme northern limit consists mainly of pastureland, and there are some pools and reedbeds here also.

*Birds*

The Sado Estuary has a varied avifauna at all times of the year, but especially so outside the breeding season, when migrant and wintering waterbirds are numerous. The area is of international importance for its wintering populations of wildfowl and waders. Noteworthy are the large numbers of Teal, Wigeon, Mallard and Shoveler. The wintering population of Black-necked Grebes (50 to 100) forms about 90% of the Portuguese population, and the same applies to Red-breasted Merganser, of which about 350 winter in the estuary. Several thousand Cormorants can also be seen in the area outside the breeding season, a reflection perhaps of the increasing use of saltpans as fish ponds.

There are also large numbers of wintering waders, particularly Avocet, Grey Plover, Ringed Plover, Dunlin, Redshank, Curlew, Black-tailed and Bar-tailed Godwits, and Snipe. Less numerous are Greenshank, Spotted Redshank and Turnstone. There is also a recently established wintering population of Black-winged Stilts. Passage brings Spoonbill, Curlew Sandpiper, Knot and various terns.

Other common wintering waterbirds include White Stork, Grey Heron, Little and Cattle Egrets, Greater Flamingo (although many also oversummer), Black-headed and Lesser Black-backed Gulls, and Sandwich Terns. Among the smaller passerines, Water Pipit, Bluethroat, Penduline Tit, and Reed Bunting, winter in small numbers.

During the breeding season, the area is somewhat quieter, due to the

Bluethroat

ASD 97

absence of large numbers of waterbirds. However, the variety of breeding birds is very interesting. White Stork, Purple Heron and Cattle and Little Egret are all fairly common in the area. Black-winged Stilts are numerous and can be seen in most saltpans and pools. Other common breeding waterbirds include Kentish Plover, Yellow-legged Gull and Little Tern.

The woodlands hold Tawny Owl, European and Red-necked Nightjars, Green, Great Spotted and Lesser Spotted Woodpeckers, Bee-eater, and Hoopoe. Both Swift and Pallid Swift are common breeding species nearby, while Alpine Swift is a passage migrant.

There are many breeding passerines. Apart from the usual, more common birds, several noteworthy species which are particularly common here include Woodlark, Cetti's Warbler, Crested Tit, Nuthatch, Bonelli's Warbler, Azure-winged Magpie, Serin, Hawfinch and Cirl Bunting,.

Surprisingly, there are few birds of prey. Buzzard, Marsh Harrier, Booted Eagle and Short-toed Eagle are seen regularly in the area, but the only other raptors seen are non-breeding visitors, such as Hen Harrier, Peregrine and Osprey.

*Accommodation*    Only 50km from Lisbon with all its facilities, Setúbal also has a wide variety of hotels. The Hotel Ibis and the Novotel are both located on the side of the road that runs from Lisbon to Alcácer do Sal. It is also possible to stay in the Tróia complex. At Alcácer do Sal there is a small pension (Residencial Silvano).

*Strategy*    Due to its large size, the Sado Estuary takes two or three days to explore thoroughly, but about 70 species can be seen in a visit of one day at any time of the year, with up to 100 on good winter days. Setúbal itself has a large colony of Pallid Swifts, best looked for in the old part of the town.

### a) Southern Bank

Starting from Setúbal, it is probably wisest (and often very rewarding) to take the car ferry to Tróia. These run very frequently. The crossing takes about 15 minutes and the ticket costs 600 Esc. for a car (including driver) and 140 Esc. for each additional passenger (in 1997). During the winter, the crossing may produce good sightings of Red-breasted Merganser, Common Scoter, Mediterranean Gull, and Razorbill, as well as Bottlenose Dolphins, which are still fairly common in this area. Avoid taking the car ferry back to Setúbal on summer weekend afternoons, because the queues may be very long. On these occasions, it may be preferable to return through Alcácer do Sal (see below).

Tróia is a large tourist complex (the trees hold Firecrest in winter). The Caldeira de Tróia is a small bay, located on the east side of the Tróia peninsula (access is via the road leading to the roman ruins). It usually holds many waders, including Curlew, Sanderling and Turnstone. Occasionally, other interesting species put in appearance, such as Spoonbill, Mediterranean and Great Black-backed Gulls (scarce in

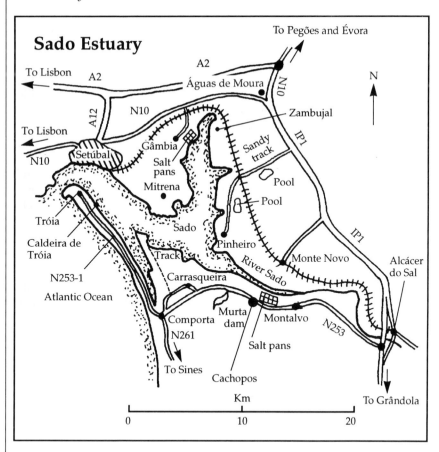

**Sado Estuary**

To Pegões and Évora

To Lisbon — A2

A2

Águas de Moura

N

N10

Zambujal

A12

N10

To Lisbon

Gâmbia

Sandy track

Setúbal

N10

Salt pans

Mitrena

Pool

Pool

Tróia

Sado

Caldeira de Tróia

Track

Pinheiro

Monte Novo

Alcácer do Sal

N253-1

Carrasqueira

River Sado

Atlantic Ocean

Comporta

Murta dam

Montalvo

N253

N261

Salt pans

To Sines

Cachopos

To Grândola

Km

0          10          20

Portugal, despite many statements to the contrary).

There is only one road south from Tróia. It leads to Comporta (about 15km to the south) and from this road one can obtain good views over the estuary; look for Greater Flamingos, wildfowl, particularly Red-breasted Mergansers, and waders, from here. Dartford Warblers are quite common throughout the Tróia peninsula, and especially so in the bushy areas. At Comporta there are large areas of saltmarsh and exposed mud flats, which often hold large numbers of waders. Avocets can often be seen here, White Storks nest in the village and Thekla Lark can be found along the road to Comporta beach.

Immediately before Comporta village, take the first road to the left after passing the rice museum (Museu do Arroz) and then immediately veer left after a small restaurant (good food!). Follow this very rough track past a group of houses and after crossing a cement irrigation channel, veer left and follow the track northwards to the end. Small reedy pools here hold Water Rail, Marsh Harriers, Penduline Tits and warblers. From the dyke around the rice fields, Red-breasted Merganser, Black-necked Grebe, Greater Flamingo and various waders can be seen in parties out in the estuary proper.

The road forks at Comporta, with one road (N261) leading away from the estuary to the south (to Lagoa de Santo André) and the other (N253) running eastwards towards Alcácer do Sal. The latter road should be followed until rice fields appear on the left. Park carefully and explore the pool (rather well hidden) that lies about 100m to the right of the road. This pool, called Murta Dam, holds a large colony of Cattle and Little Egrets; a few Little Bitterns and Purple Herons also occur, along with Night and Squacco Herons (the latter has bred). Booted and Short-toed Eagles are regular here, mainly during the breeding season, while Great Spotted Cuckoos often display in late winter and early spring. Breeding passerines include Great Reed Warbler, Serin and Iberian Chiffchaff and in winter this is a good place to see Penduline Tit and waterfowl.

Carrying on to Alcácer do Sal, there are many areas of saltpans lying to the north of the road, close to the estuary. These saltpans often hold interesting waders, especially at high tide, including Black-winged Stilt, Kentish Plover and Spotted Redshank. They can be reached by following one of the tracks to the northern side of the road, but care should be taken as some of them include stretches with deep sand.

The area that extends to the south of this road forms the largest stand of Umbrella Pine in Portugal. The variety of birds is low, but a few interesting species are quite common, particularly Crested Tit, Short-toed Treecreeper, Woodchat Shrike, Azure-winged Magpie, and Serin.

The town of Alcácer do Sal has large numbers of breeding White Storks, mainly in the church towers and in the castle. Crossing the bridge which is close to the centre, look for a reedbed island in the river. Cattle and Little Egrets sometimes roost here, while Great Reed Warblers are ubiquitous in summer.

## b) Northern Bank

To explore this area, leave Setúbal on the N10 eastwards, towards Águas de Moura and Alcácer do Sal. Along the first 15km, there are many complexes of saltpans off to the right-hand side of the road, which often hold parties of waders and breeding Black-winged Stilts, Kentish Plovers and Little Terns. The saltpans around Mitrena, Praias do Sado and Gâmbia are particularly worth exploring. Follow signs for 'Zona industrial', Praias do Sado and Gâmbia, respectively.

Further east, close to km 53, there is another road to the right with a signpost, rather unclearly marked, reading Zambujal, which leads to an area of reedbeds, rice fields and saltmarsh. Here again there are Black-winged Stilts, as well as Iberian Yellow Wagtail, Fan-tailed and Cetti's and Great Reed Warblers in summer. Outside the breeding season there are many waders, as well as Bluethroat, Dartford Warbler and Penduline Tit.

About 5km south of Águas de Moura there is a sandy track to the right (passable throughout the year) signposted Pinheiro, which leads through woodland for about 10km. The track passes through an area of dense woods of Cork Oaks and pines, which hold large numbers of Woodlarks, Crested Tits, three species of woodpecker, Firecrest (in winter), Rock Sparrow and Cirl Buntings and leads to a small village close to the river. This is a very interesting area with a rich bird life and it is well worth walking a circuit around the village of Pinheiro. There are extensive rice fields, which hold feeding Cattle and Little Egrets and White Storks, many Black-winged Stilts (also a few wintering birds), wintering Peregrine, Water Pipits, Bluethroats and several warblers. Close to the riverbank, there are extensive mudflats, which hold large flocks of passage and wintering waterbirds, including Greater Flamingo, Avocet, Curlew and Greenshank.

# 11  Santo André Lagoon

Santo André Lagoon is one of the largest lakes in western Portugal and although at present it is not afforded a large degree of protection, it still forms an important wetland area at all times of the year. The lagoon lies in the dunes of the western Alentejo. Its coastal location and its vegetation make it very important during migration time, with large numbers of migrating waders and passerines in the area. An annual ringing project here in autumn has revealed that the area is used by large numbers of migrant passerines.

*Location*

This site lies about 120km south of Lisbon on the west coast of Portugal. Full details of the area can be found on the following maps: 1:100,000: 42; 1:50,000: 42-A; 1:25,000: 505.

*Description*

The lake itself covers about 600ha in winter, but the management regime produces a series of seasonal changes in water level, salinity and productivity, which are reflected in a wide variety of bird life. An important part of the eastern shore is covered by aquatic vegetation, formed by reedmace, reeds and willows. The lake is separated from the sea by a large chain of sand dunes covered mainly with Maritime Pines and low dense scrub. Further inland, the soil is still composed largely of sand and considerable woodlands exist, dominated mainly by plantations of Maritime Pine and Cork Oak, with few cultivated areas.

Human activities vary according to the time of year and like many other wetlands in southern Europe, it is under threat from a variety of sources. Pressure resulting from tourism can be heavy in summer and although people concentrate largely along the northern part of the lake, there are no means to prevent access to the southern part and disturbance can result. In winter, hunting is a problem, as the area is full of waterfowl but there is little control on illegal shooting. An enormous legalised collective 'shoot' takes place every year on November 1st.

*Birds*

The richest months are March, April, August and September, as the number of species is augmented by passage birds, many of which are trans-saharan migrants, though each season has its own specialities.

In some winters, the lake holds a wide variety of dabbling ducks, including Mallard, Teal, Shoveler, Pintail and Gadwall. Up to five-hundred Red-crested Pochard can be seen at times and Coot counts exceed 10,000. During officially monitored 'shoots', Crested Coot has been found. Penduline Tits and Water Pipits are also regular in winter, and because of the mild conditions (with temperatures below 10° C rare) sightings of White Storks and Hoopoes are commonplace. Other interesting wintering species have included Squacco Heron, Glossy Ibis and Richard's Pipit.

Spring comes very early here and by mid-February hirundines are common. Great Spotted Cuckoos are seen from mid-February onwards and warm anti-cyclonic conditions in March can bring early passages of Garganey, Short-toed Larks, Yellow Wagtails, Woodchat Shrikes, and singing Sedge and Willow Warblers. Spring arrivals are much dependent upon weather conditions and throughout April and May falls of migrants may occur which in recent years have included White-winged Black Tern and Roller. By this time the reed beds are vibrating with the songs of Savi's, Reed and Great Reed Warblers and at dusk Little Bitterns can be heard 'barking'.

Summer is usually a noisy time at the lake with young birds everywhere and, though migration is almost non-existent, locally breeding Black-winged Stilts, Bee-eaters and hirundines can be common. Hobbies breed nearby and can often be seen scything through the masses of hirundines at dusk. Crested Tits, Hawfinches and Cirl Buntings are common in the surrounding woods.

Autumn movement begins in July with a few early returning Holarctic waders and the migration of ducks and Coot from Spain to moult at the lake. From August to November, heavy passage has been recorded and most trans-saharan migrants can be seen in variable numbers; rarities have included Audouin's Gull and Red-necked Phalarope.

*Accommodation*

It is possible to reach the area in 2 hours from Lisbon or 1.5 hours from Setúbal and, of course, these cities offer a wide variety of pensions and hotels. There is a small hotel in Costa de Santo André and pensions or cottages can be found in Melides and Sines nearby. Accommodation can be arranged in advance through travel agencies.

*Strategy*

When coming from Lisbon, take the A2 southwards to Setúbal. On reaching this town, follow the signs to the port and take the Tróia ferry boat. The route from Tróia is fairly straightforward, southwards through Comporta and then for 11 kilometres until signs indicate a right turn for Melides and Sines. This road passes by Melides village; about 5km further on take a road to the right indicating Lagoa de Santo André. Veer left at the first major turning, which goes through Brescos village. For the next kilometre all tracks to the right will lead to the lake; they are sandy and negotiable throughout most of the year.

In the morning, the best vantage point is a small hillock overlooking the lake. Approach this by taking the first turn right (track A on the map) at a small bridge just past Brescos. This route brings you through cultivated fields, between two cottages to the eastern shore of the lake, from where wildfowl can be watched.

Return to the main road, and after a few hundred metres veer right again. This track (track B on the map) leads to a place that lies between the open lake and the reedbed, which can be good for passerines including Bluethroat and Water Pipit in autumn/winter and dusk movements of herons.

Proceeding southwards on the main road take the second next right turn (track C) which leads through pines and Cork Oak to the

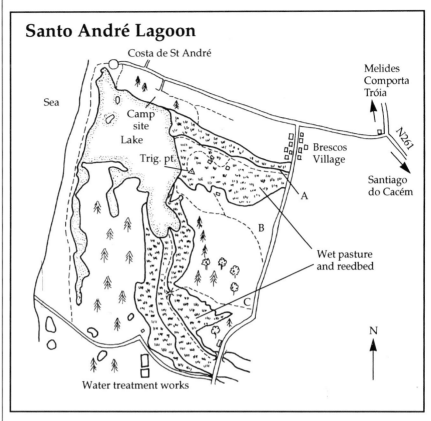

**Santo André Lagoon**

Costa de St André

Sea

Camp site

Lake

Trig. pt.

Brescos Village

Melides Comporta Tróia

N261

Santiago do Cacém

A

B

Wet pasture and reedbed

C

N

Water treatment works

south-eastern corner of the lake. Park here and walk westwards to a small cement bridge. The area is very good in summer for breeding warblers and in winter for Penduline Tits and wildfowl. Turn at the bridge and following the track north walk to the heart of the main reedbeds; depending on water level and season, this area can be excellent for waders and terns. The surrounding reed beds are good for Great Reed and Savi's Warblers, Bluethroat and Penduline Tit (the latter two in winter).

Towards the end of the day, take the tarred road at the extreme southern end of the lake west towards the sea. Park very carefully about 2km along this road, where glimpses of the lake can be had and walk north along the sandy tracks between the pines parallel to the western shore of the lake. This eventually brings you to relatively undisturbed rich lake vegetation, where superb views can be obtained eastwards over the lake. Over one thousand egrets roost here and the calling of Stone-curlews is constant.

On busy weekend evenings, when the queues for the returning ferries are despairingly long, it may be preferable to drive along the N120 via Alcácer do Sal and then follow the IP1 back to Lisbon.

## 12 Elvas Plains and Upper River Guadiana

The Elvas area was formerly regarded as one of the best places in Portugal for open-country species. Nowadays, the situation has changed markedly as intensification of agriculture has led to increased disturbance and habitat changes. Furthermore, a motorway crossing the area is at present under construction. Nevertheless, the area holds one of the richest bird communities in Portugal and it is still possible to find here most of the species one would expect in southern Portugal, including waterbirds, soaring birds, birds of the steppe, and small passerines.

*Location*

The Elvas area lies due east of Lisbon, in the eastern Alentejo, very close to the Spanish border. Lying directly on the Lisbon-Madrid road, Elvas can easily be reached from Lisbon (via the A2 and A6 and then the N4) and is also strategically located for those entering or leaving the country by car. Full details of the area can be found on the following maps: 1:100,000: 33 and 37; 1:50,000: 33-C and 37-A; 1:25,000: 400, 401, 413, 414 and 428.

*Description*

The area lies close to the Spanish border where the River Guadiana enters Portugal. Near Elvas, the frontier is marked by the river and by its tributary the Caia. Both rivers have flat and very fertile valleys. Elvas is a medium-sized town that has grown markedly in the last few years. The old part of the town is still surrounded by a large wall built to protect the inhabitants from attacks in historical times.

The riverine vegetation is very rich, with many Poplars and Eucalyptus, dense bushes and some reedbeds. The larger tributaries have similar vegetation, while the small streams are lined with Genista and Oleander, especially around Campo Maior.

Agriculture, which is both intensive and extensive, predominates and there are large irrigation systems, with huge expanses of rice, sunflower and corn fields. Away from the river, wheat predominates, but the existing woodland groves, consisting mainly of Olive and Holm Oak, are an important feature of the area. Although the landscape is relatively flat around Elvas, as one moves southwards the contours alter gradually, with some steep, rocky slopes and dense bushy cover.

The Caia dam, built directly on the River Caia a few kilometres to the north of Elvas, forms the largest reservoir in this region, while small dams have been built here and there, mainly for water storage and irrigation.

*Birds*

This area is particularly important for breeding birds, being most interesting in spring and early summer. Widespread and easy to find are White Stork, Bee-eater, Hoopoe, Great Grey and Woodchat Shrikes, Spotless Starling, and Serin. Cattle Egret and Little Egret are also numerous, however during the breeding season they concentrate at their breeding colonies.

Sadly, steppe birds have declined dramatically in recent years, due mainly to intensification of agriculture, which has destroyed much of their natural habitat. Little Bustard and Stone-curlew can still be seen, but Great Bustard is very scarce and Black-bellied Sandgrouse is apparently extinct. However, the Elvas plains are probably the most reliable area in Portugal for Roller and one of the few places where this bird can be said to be common. The rice fields here hold some of the most accessible colonies of Collared Pratincole in the country, together with numerous Black-winged Stilts and a few Little Ringed Plovers.

Birds of prey are not numerous: Montagu's Harrier, Buzzard and Kestrel are the only common species, while Black and Black-shouldered Kites, and Short-toed and Booted Eagles have a more restricted distribution. Lesser Kestrel does not appear to breed here any more, although it is still widespread in the Spanish city of Badajoz, just across the border and flocks are seen on occasion hunting on the Portuguese side.

The variety of passerines here is diverse with five species of lark breeding: Calandra, Short-toed, Wood, Crested and Thekla. The latter two are common, giving an excellent opportunity to compare both species. Crag Martins and Red-rumped Swallows have a very localised distribution but can be found at specific places (see below). The list of breeding warblers is also interesting: Fan-tailed, Cetti's, Great Reed, Melodious and Sardinian Warblers are all fairly common and easy to find. The area also holds several species that are less common or more localised, such as Little Bittern, Great Spotted Cuckoo, Azure-winged Magpie, Rock Sparrow and Penduline Tit.

Common Waxbill, an introduced species, is common in reedbeds and riverine vegetation along the Guadiana and Caia valleys. Red Avadavat (another introduced bird) occurs in the same areas as the Waxbill, although the two species do not normally form mixed flocks.

In mid-summer, the area has large post-breeding concentrations of White Storks (up to 1000 birds), while many northern European waders use the rice fields as a feeding area during their southward migration. The riverine vegetation is often used by migrant passerines.

In winter, most of the breeding birds are absent. Nevertheless, it is possible to find interesting residents. Large flocks of Little Bustards often occur and Black-shouldered Kite is regular. There are also four species of larks still present. Winter visitors include Common Crane, Red Kite and Hen Harrier.

*Accommodation*

Elvas has a variety of types of accommodation. The Hotel Dom Luís lies directly on the N4, and there is also a pousada a few hundred metres to the east. Outside the town, on the road to Spain there is another hotel, called the Hotel Brasa. It is also possible (and a good deal less expensive) to find smaller pensions in the old part of the town or in Campo Maior, which lies a few kilometres to the north.

As it lies on one of the main roads between Spain and Portugal, there are a lot of restaurants, both in Elvas, in Caia and along the roadside.

*Strategy*

In Elvas itself, there are good numbers of breeding Common and Pallid Swifts. These species do not usually form mixed colonies, but in this town they breed not far from each other, thus allowing a direct comparison between them. One of the best watch points for these species is the Praça 25 de Abril, which lies at the western end of the old part of the town, just in front of the bank Totta & Açores. The best time of day to look for swifts here is in the early morning or in late afternoon.

The surrounding countryside is worth exploring in all directions. The best sites are all within 20km of Elvas and are easy to visit. The following are suggested itineraries.

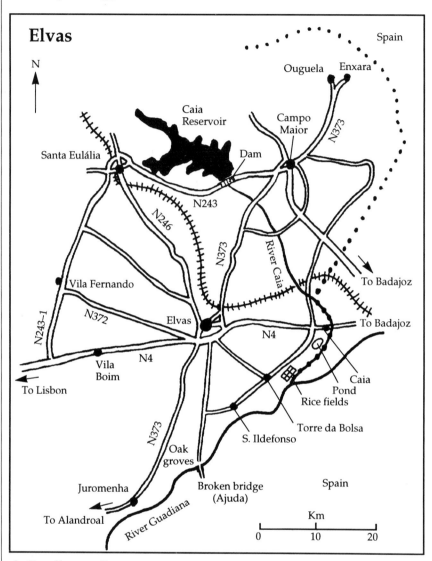

## a) Guadiana valley

Leave Elvas on the N4 towards Spain. Immediately after passing an old castle on the right-hand side, veer right on a minor road signposted Torre de Bolsa. This road leads to one of the best areas in spring and summer. After passing some olive groves (which hold Serin, Short-toed Treecreeper and Woodchat Shrike) you enter an area of open fields, which have Montagu's Harrier, Little Bustard, Quail, Bee-eater, Roller, Fan-tailed Warbler and Southern Grey Shrike. Stone-curlews are best looked for in the evening or at dusk, when they are calling. The elusive Great Bustard has been seen here. After about 6.5km, the road ends at a T-junction, beside two houses. A rough track leads straight ahead through sunflower fields, which have Crested and Short-toed Larks, to the river Guadiana, which here forms the border with Spain. The riverine vegetation is rich. Penduline Tits bred here in 1994, in riverine reeds. Other species here include Little Egret, Little Bittern, Cetti's, Great Reed and Melodious Warblers, Golden Oriole, Serin, and Common Waxbill.

Returning to the T-junction, turn right (east) and after 2km turn right again on the first large track. This leads to extensive rice fields, where Black-winged Stilt and Collared Pratincole breed in good numbers, along with Little Ringed Plover and abundant Crested Larks. Bee-eaters are often seen hawking for insects here. Autumn passage begins in July with Ruff, Redshank, Green and Common Sandpipers, and Black-tailed Godwit feeding in the rice fields, often surrounded by hundreds of White Storks. Proceeding to the river, there is a reedbed with Cetti's and Great Reed Warblers, along with Common Waxbill and Red Avadavat. There are more rice fields to the east, near Alfarófia and Caia, where the road reaches the N4.

To the south of Elvas lies another interesting area called Ajuda. Look for the road to Ajuda, which passes near the Bombeiros (fire brigade station) and reaches the river Guadiana after about 10km, ending near a broken stone bridge. This area can also be reached from Torre de Bolsa, by following the road to the west and veering left at the T-junction. The landscape is attractive here and the river is good for Little Egret, while the Holm Oaks just to the north hold Stone-curlew, Hoopoe, Woodlark, Thekla Lark, Sardinian Warbler, Short-toed Treecreeper, and Serin.

## b) Elvas north and west

About 15km west of Elvas lies an area of open fields. Take the N372, which leaves Elvas directly from the aqueduct and proceed to Vila Fernando. From there, explore westwards (N372) and southwards (N243-1), taking one of the small tracks that leads into the open fields. Breeding birds here include Black Kite, Montagu's Harrier, Short-toed Eagle, Quail, Collared Pratincole (scarce), Roller, Crested and Calandra Larks, Fan-tailed Warbler, Melodious Warbler, and Southern Grey and Woodchat Shrikes. About 2km south of Vila Fernando there is a pool close to the right-hand side of the road, with Black-winged Stilt and Little Ringed Plover in summer.

To explore northwards, take the N373 to Campo Maior (watch for Roller and Montagu's Harrier on the way). If coming from Caia, take the minor road to the north signposted Campo Maior and after about 2km stop as there are many reedbeds which hold Great Reed Warbler in summer. From Campo Maior, the N243 leads westwards to the Barragem do Caia, a large reservoir used in winter by various wildfowl. However, in summer it is worth spending a few minutes on the middle of the dam looking downstream: Crag Martin, Red-rumped Swallow and Spotless Starling all breed in the wall of the dam, while Little Bittern has been seen on the small pool just under it. To the north-east of Campo Maior, the N373 leads to Ouguela. Just before reaching Ouguela, take the right-hand road to Enxara and cross the river. Species here include Great Spotted Cuckoo, Crested Lark, Crag Martin, Melodious Warbler, Spotless Starling, and Serin. The surrounding Holm

Oaks have Azure-winged Magpie and Rock Sparrow. The castle of Ouguela can be used in winter as a watching point in late afternoon, as Common Cranes move to their roosts.

# 13 Mourão

Around the town of Mourão, close to the Spanish border, lies an open, unprotected area with largely uncultivated fields. Despite the intensification of agriculture that has caused a reduction of most steppe birds in the Alentejo, Mourão has remained a 'secret corner', where relict populations of several endangered species have survived. Its steppe birds are of particular interest and it is the best site in Portugal for Black-bellied Sandgrouse.

*Location*

The site lies to the south-east of Évora in south-eastern Portugal, close to the Spanish border. Full details of the area can be found on the following maps: 1:100,000: 41; 1:50,000: 41-A and 41-C; 1:25,000: 474 and 483.

*Description*

The area lies on the eastern side of the River Guadiana, one of the three largest catchments in the country. The river valley is V-shaped here, and the slopes are covered with Olive trees and bushes.

This river nowadays faces very serious problems with water pollution, which is mainly caused by agriculture and a cellulose factory. Furthermore, there is a threat of inundation, due to the building of a giant dam called Barragem do Alqueva, which will completely fill the valley for over 50km and flood the surrounding area. This project is moving slowly but is likely to produce profound long term changes.

Away from the river valley, the landscape is rather flat and open. Due to the poverty of the soil, the pattern of cultivated fields varies between years and therefore large areas are left undisturbed. Woodland consists mainly of Olive and Holm Oaks groves. A few reservoirs can be found here and there and are used for irrigation purposes.

*Birds*

Mourão has long been famous in Portugal for its steppe and open-country species. Although many of the birds that can be seen here occur over most of the Alentejo province, some of them are more easily found in this area than anywhere else in Portugal. One of the highlights of Mourão is Black-bellied Sandgrouse. This bird is fairly common and the site is possibly the only place in Portugal where this species is 'guaranteed'. Stone-curlew is widespread and Great and Little Bustards occur in the area, while in spring Calandra Larks can be found singing everywhere.

The area is also quite good for birds of prey: regular species during the breeding season include Black-shouldered Kite, Buzzard, Black Kite, Montagu's Harrier, Short-toed and Booted Eagles. Black Stork and Egyptian Vulture are scarce, while Black Vulture is seen occasionally.

The existing reservoirs hold several breeding waterbirds, of which Little Ringed Plover and Black-winged Stilt are probably the most interesting ones.

Black-bellied
Sandgrouse

Antony S. Disley 97

Summer visitors to the area include Great Spotted Cuckoo (best looked for in late-February and March), Quail, Bee-eater, Roller, Short-toed Lark, Red-rumped Swallow, Black-eared Wheatear, Subalpine and Melodious Warblers, Golden Oriole and Rufous Bushchat. Most nests of White Stork hold small colonies of Spanish Sparrows, which also breeds in large numbers in wooded areas.

Winter can be exciting at Mourão, with several thousand Common Cranes roosting in the area. Flocks can often be seen feeding in the fields and oak groves or flying over in the evening, forming large 'letters' in the sky. Red Kites and Hen Harriers are also regular non-breeding visitors in the area, while Dotterel has been recorded on passage. Of course the resident passerines, such as Crag Martin, Spotless Starling and Rock Sparrow, also remain in the area.

*Accommodation*     If you visit the Elvas area (see previous site), then it is possible to reach Mourão in about one hour, returning to Elvas in the evening. If you plan to stay in this area, there is a hotel in Monsaraz and pensions in Reguengos de Monsaraz and Mourão. If there are no rooms available, try Évora, which lies just 55km to the north-west and has a variety of accommodation facilities.

*Strategy*     Starting from Évora, take the N18 and then the N256 eastwards through Reguengos de Monsaraz and proceed to Mourão village. From here there are roads to many sites, allowing exploration of most of the area.

### a) São Leonardo
Locate the graveyard at the eastern end of Mourão and take the road to the left, which is signposted Espanha (Spain) to the left. This route (N256-1) runs eastwards to a hamlet called São Leonardo. The passport

control here was withdrawn a few years ago and there are normally no problems crossing and recrossing the frontier. It is possible to park the car in São Leonardo and begin birdwatching in Portugal. However, it is probably better to cross the border and take the first surfaced road to the left, which leads through open fields to a pond where there is often a variety of waterfowl.

This area deserves a long careful circuit on foot, especially across the uncultivated fields, which form the main habitat for Black-bellied Sandgrouse. Park on the other side of the reservoir and walk over the plains. In summer, this area can also provide Lesser Kestrel, Black Kite, Quail, Roller and Short-toed Lark, while Black-shouldered Kite, Stone Curlew, Great and Little Bustards and Calandra Larks can be seen all year round. The reservoir itself sometimes has Little Egrets and in winter, there are normally flocks of Common Cranes feeding and flying around, which should not be disturbed.

Returning to the N256-1, drive back and take one of the rough tracks to the left (southwards). These lead through open fields and Holm Oak groves and in summer can provide a good selection of birds, such as Booted Eagle, Great Spotted Cuckoo, Black-eared Wheatear, Rock Sparrow and Azure-winged Magpie. A few small reservoirs exist here and can hold Black-winged Stilt and Little Ringed Plover. The Holm Oak groves hold large colonies of Spanish Sparrows, although these tend to move from one year to the next and a careful search may be needed.

### b) Ferrarias

This area lies to the north of Mourão and can be reached on an unmarked narrow surfaced road that runs from Mourão past the Mourão reservoir and leads to an uninhabited area with excellent birds (if you can't find your way, just ask someone for Ferrarias). The road crosses an area of open fields which are excellent for soaring birds of prey, including Montagu's Harrier, Black Kite and Short-toed Eagle in summer. Black-bellied Sandgrouse also occurs here, but patient listening is essential. Other birds here include White Stork, Stone-curlew, Little Bustard and Bee-eater. Proceeding along the road, which becomes unsurfaced after a while, it is worth stopping near two abandoned houses beside a small Eucalyptus wood. The surrounding Holm Oaks hold Black-shouldered Kite, Great Spotted Cuckoo, Hoopoe (numerous), Crested and Thekla Larks (permitting critical comparison), Black-eared Wheatear, Southern Grey and Woodchat Shrikes and Rock Sparrow.

### c) Southern sector

From Mourão, take the road that leads southwards (signposted Póvoa) and stop after 8km at the bridge over the Alcarrache River. This site holds several interesting species, such as Bee-eater, Crag Martin, Red-rumped Swallow, Melodious Warbler and Spanish Sparrow. A walk along the river may produce Eagle Owl, but this bird is, as usual, difficult to locate.

Just north of the bridge over the Alcarrache River there is a crossing where a road leads to Luz (signposted). By following this road for a few km and taking one of the rough tracks to the left, you will pass some olive groves and reach open fields which hold Quail, Little Bustard, Roller, Calandra Lark and, with luck, Black-bellied Sandgrouse.

The road that leads from Luz back to Mourão is usually a reliable site for Roller (look for them on the telegraph wires along the road).

## 14 Barrancos

The village of Barrancos is a Portuguese village with some Spanish traditions where the patois is a mixture of Spanish and Portuguese. It is the only place in the country where bull fights end with the death of the animal. The surrounding area is relatively undisturbed, as the density of inhabitants is among the lowest in Portugal. Lying in such a remote corner, the region offers unparalleled conditions for large soaring birds and there are also many interesting woodland birds.

*Location*    The village of Barrancos lies in south-east Portugal in the eastern corner of the southern Alentejo, very close to the Spanish border. Full details of the area can be found on the following maps: 1:100,000: 44; 1:50,000: 44-A, 44-B and 44-CD; 1:25,000: 503, 504, 514 and 515.

*Description*

There are no towns or villages between Amareleja or Safara, to the west, and Barrancos, to the east, with only a few houses scattered throughout the area. Consequently, the region has not suffered badly from changes wrought by man. It is hilly and wooded, with Holm Oaks the most conspicuous tree, while sun rose is found where woods give way to dense scrub. The Ardila and Murtigão rivers run westwards through the area, before entering the Guadiana, forming unusually narrow, deep and relatively undisturbed valleys where nature appears as it may have been centuries ago. Its value in terms of biodiversity and scarce species can be compared to the much larger International Tagus and Douro valleys. The dryness of the soil and the low population density has produced a kind of 'desertification' although cattle grazing is an important activity and the famous black pigs of the Alentejo can be found here. From the conservation point of view, this area is very important and its bird-life is one of the richest in Portugal away from the coast.

*Birds*

This is a good site for birds of prey and vultures. Griffon Vultures are quite common and flocks of up to 20 birds are regularly seen, sometimes with one or two Black Vultures among them. Furthermore, this is the only area in southern Portugal where Red Kites can be said to be common, especially in winter. Other common or fairly common breeding raptors are Black Kite, Montagu's Harrier, Short-toed Eagle and Buzzard, while Black-shouldered Kite is scarce. Finally there are one or two pairs of Bonelli's and Golden Eagles, but these birds are scarce and endangered. This is also one of the few places in Portugal where sightings of Imperial Eagle regularly occur. Black Storks are another speciality of this region and can sometimes be seen flying over the valleys, while the elusive Eagle Owl often calls at dusk from late winter onwards and is sometimes heard in the more remote valleys.

Apart from its large soaring birds, Barrancos is also outstanding for its small land birds. Common species in the Holm Oak areas include Bee-eater, Thekla Lark, Woodlark, Black-eared Wheatear, Subalpine and Orphean Warblers, Woodchat Shrike, Azure-winged Magpie, and Rock Sparrow. In the deep rocky valleys there are Red-rumped Swallow, Crag Martin, Blue Rock Thrush, Raven, Hawfinch, and Rock Bunting, while in the old castle of Noudar there are breeding Black Redstarts.

Around Amareleja, the landscape is more open and it is possible to find White Stork, Roller, Great Spotted Cuckoo and Golden Oriole in late spring and early summer. Amareleja and Safara are two of the best sites for wintering Common Cranes in Portugal, which feed in open Holm Oak woods over most of the region. Red Kites are also regular in winter here.

*Accommodation*

Unfortunately, most of the tiny villages have no hotels and only one or two small pensions, such as those at Barrancos. It may be necessary to try one of the larger towns, such as Moura, which lies 50km to the west of Barrancos. Otherwise, it may be necessary to stay at Évora (110km to the north west) and leave from there at dawn.

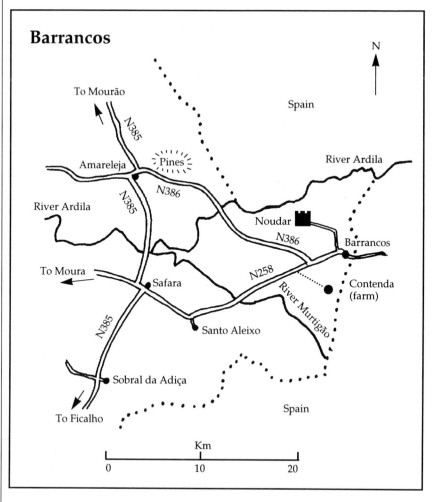

**Barrancos**

N

To Mourão

Spain

N385

Amareleja

Pines

River Ardila

N386

River Ardila

N385

Noudar

N386

Barrancos

To Moura

Safara

N258

Contenda
(farm)

River Murtigão

N385

Santo Aleixo

Sobral da Adiça

Spain

To Ficalho

Km

0      10      20

*Strategy*

There are two roads leading to the area, both coming from the west –
one from Amareleja (N386) and the other from Safara (N258), forming a
triangle of considerable interest.

Begin by exploring the area around Amareleja. Just to the north of the
village, there is a small bridge with some Holm Oaks where Rollers are
regularly seen. Leaving on the N386 eastwards, stop at the cemetery just
before a plantation of Umbrella Pines; this is a good place to find Great
Spotted Cuckoo, Red-rumped Swallow and Golden Oriole in summer.

Proceeding eastwards on the N386, there is a bridge near km 47.5 over
the river Ardila. This site is also worth a stop, as Red-rumped Swallow,
Sardinian and Melodious Warblers, Azure-winged Magpie and
Hawfinch can all seen from the bridge. From here eastwards, Griffon
Vultures are commonly seen. Furthermore, a walk northwards along the
river valley may produce Bonelli's Eagle and other birds of prey.

The road continues eastwards, through Holm Oaks. Stop after a few
kilometres and explore near the road. Breeding species here include
Bee-eater, Woodlark, Thekla Lark, Short-toed Treecreeper, Woodchat
Shrike and Spotless Starling.

On arriving at Barrancos, turn left at the petrol station, following a narrow surfaced road that is signposted Noudar. After 3km, stop at the bridge over the river Murtega. Crag Martin, Red-rumped Swallow, Blue Rock Thrush and Rock Bunting are all possible here. After crossing the bridge, take the left fork and proceed for about 10km to the old castle of Noudar. The road is not surfaced, but is in fairly good condition, and leads through extensive Holm Oaks, which have Bee-eater, Black-eared Wheatear, Azure-winged Magpie, Rock Sparrow and Orphean Warbler as breeding species. The castle of Noudar has Crag Martin, Red-rumped Swallow and Black Redstart. The tower in the middle of the castle is an excellent watching point for large soaring birds, including Black Stork, large vultures and the occasional Golden and Imperial Eagles. The best time to see them is around noon. The area around the castle is worth a detailed examination and after dusk this is a good site for Eagle Owl, with calling birds being recorded annually.

Back at Barrancos, leave westwards on the N258 towards Safara and Moura and turn left near km 97 to the farm of Contenda. Vultures have survived until recently because they were regularly fed by the Forestry Service. Griffons are usually seen in considerable numbers, often with a few Black Vultures among them. Eagle Owl and Orphean Warbler also occur here.

# 15 Castro Verde and Mértola

This extensive area contains the largest expanse of uncultivated plains in southern Portugal. Although not officially protected, efforts are being made to conserve part or all of this valuable area. The Castro Verde plains are undoubtedly the best refugia for steppe birds in Portugal, offering the visitor a unique opportunity to see several very rare or endangered birds, including some species with the dubious distinction of being in the Red Data Book.

*Location*

This site lies to the south of Beja in southern Portugal. Full details of the area can be found on the following maps: 1:100,000: 46; 1:50,000: 46-A, B, C and D; 1:25,000: Castro Verde: 539, 548 and 549; Mértola: 550, 558 and 559.

*Description*

This is an impressive steppe-like area, where the rolling plains form a vast ocean of undulating grass and wheat. Cultivated fields alternate with uncultivated ones as, due to the dryness of the soil, fields ploughed one year are left fallow the next. Woodlands are almost absent in this area and are restricted to a few Holm Oak woods, most of which lie far from the main roads. They have been cleared of the original understorey, once formed by Sun Rose. Here and there, small Eucalyptus plantations break the monotonous landscape and there are some tiny plantations of olive trees. The main roads are bordered with Eucalyptus trees.

As in the rest of eastern Portugal, the 'flight from the land' has concentrated the Alentejo's ageing population in the existing villages and small towns. Most isolated houses have been abandoned and, in some cases, are in a state of advanced decay. Almodôvar, Castro Verde and Mértola are the only 'large' towns in this strange and beautiful place.

The River Guadiana runs just past Mértola, but its valley is very deep and dry here and is rather devoid of aquatic vegetation, at least when compared with the more flat sections further north, around Moura and Elvas. However, in the smaller river valleys the vegetation is richer; Sedge and Oleander abound, and there are often a few other trees such as Ash and Poplar.

East of Mértola, the soil is even drier, the area is semi-arid in biogeographical terms and the cultivated areas are restricted. Sun Rose is the dominant wild species of plant and forms large uniform patches. At Mina de S. Domingos there are extensive ruins of an old abandoned copper mine, nowadays full of leached sulphate deposits, with many Oleanders and Eucalyptus. The whole place has a character unlike any other in Portugal, part Mediterranean scrubland, part multicoloured lunar landscape.

*Birds*

The area is very important for species that are quite rare in the rest of Portugal. This is probably the best area in the country to look for Lesser Kestrel, Great Bustard, Rufous Bushchat and Spectacled Warbler. Other species found on the plains throughout the year are White Stork, Little Bustard, Stone-curlew, Calandra and Thekla Larks, and Raven. Black-bellied Sandgrouse breeds in the area, but is now very rare, probably due to increasing disturbance, hunting activities and intensification of agriculture.

Rufous Bushchat

In summer, one can find a wide variety of interesting migrant breeding species. The common birds include Black Kite, Montagu's Harrier, Red-necked Nightjar, Roller, Bee-eater, Short-toed Lark, Red-rumped Swallow, Black-eared Wheatear, Woodchat Shrike, Golden Oriole and Spanish Sparrow, all of which are fairly widespread. Less

common are Pallid Swift, Tawny Pipit, Orphean and Subalpine
Warblers.

In winter, the plains are full of Lapwings, Golden Plovers, and
Skylarks, sometimes with a few Hen Harriers and the odd Red Kite.
This is one of the four main sites for wintering Common Cranes in
Portugal (the others being at Évora, Elvas and Mourão) and up to 200
of these birds can be seen regularly flying over the plains in the
evening.

*Accommodation*    Accommodation facilities are limited, but there are a few hotels in
the area, none of them very costly and, although modest and small,
they are generally good value for money. In Castro Verde, there is the
Pensão Costa. It is not very expensive and lies in the centre of the
village, but it does not have private bathrooms. The more expensive
Aparthotel do Castro has small apartments and is more comfortable. In
Mértola there are two or three places to stay. Alternatively, it is possible
to base oneself in Beja, a larger town lying about 40 minutes drive to
the north.

Castro Verde and Mértola have several restaurants, some of them
excellent.

*Strategy*    Castro Verde can be reached from Lisbon via the A2 and then the
IP1 to Alvalade, taking the N261 to Aljustrel and finally the N2 to
Castro Verde. The area is rather uniform, and this means that for many
species there are no specific sites due to the large amount of habitat
available. It is therefore wise to explore the area as a whole, rather than
fixing on any given site. While driving, occasionally glance up at the
telegraph wires, which are frequently used as a perch site by Bee-eaters,
Black-eared Wheatears, shrikes and, sometimes, Rollers.

The N123, which runs from Castro Verde eastwards to Mértola, can

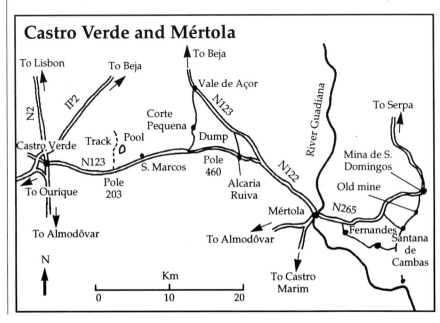

# Castro Verde and Mértola

be used as a working base for exploratory runs. Most birds can be seen along the road or within viewing distance of it. This road has little traffic, making it a rather quiet and pleasant place for birdwatching, though care needs to be taken in parking safely. The road is lined by numbered telegraph poles (starting with pole no. 1 at Castro Verde), enabling easy referencing (recently some were removed).

There is a track which leaves the road northwards from pole 203 signposted Apariça, which can be travelled by car, except after heavy rain. This track crosses the plains (offering good chances of seeing all the mentioned steppe birds, especially Calandra Lark) and leads to a small river called Ribeira de Cobres, a good site for Rufous Bushchat and Cetti's and Melodious Warblers. Purple Heron and Black Stork have also been seen here.

Close to pole 470 there is a dump, which often has goods birds, such as White Stork (often in some numbers), Black Kite, and Raven. Poles 450 to 500 hold nests of White Storks, under which there are sometimes nests of Spanish Sparrows. These birds breed elsewhere in the area, both under isolated nests of White Stork and in woodland.

Most sightings of Black-bellied Sandgrouse in Portugal are from this area or around Mourão. However, sightings cannot be assured, and the best chance of finding them seems to be to walk, rather than to drive, through the plains, especially over uncultivated fields.

Apart from being scenically unique, the village of Mértola is very interesting, and also holds Portugal's largest colony of Lesser Kestrels. Almost all the birds breed in the Convento de S. Francisco just outside Mértola itself, where the colony is carefully monitored and protected by the owners. The convent itself is a wildlife refuge and art centre, the artwork drawing its inspiration from the surrounding wildlife. On entering the convent, it is necessary to ask for permission to watch the falcons and disturbance of any kind will not be tolerated. Other species breeding at Mértola include White Stork, Blue Rock Thrush and Golden Oriole.

It is also worth crossing the River Guadiana at Mértola and driving a few kilometres to the east on the N265, turning right after about 4km on a minor road that leads past Fernandes and Tamejoso. This area is good for Spectacled Warbler, a rare breeding species in Portugal. Other summer visitors include Red-rumped Swallow, Subalpine and Orphean Warblers, and Woodchat Shrike. Further east lies the Mina de S. Domingos, best approached from the tiny village of Santana de Cambas. At the village, look for Pallid Swifts and head north along rough stony trails, through Sun Rose scrub (a good habitat for Subalpine Warbler), towards the chimneys of the old mine, just visible in the distance. Black-bellied Sandgrouse, Rock Bunting, Roller and Thekla Lark are regular. The old mine has many Crag Martins and Red-rumped Swallows and a few Black-eared Wheatears. White-rumped Swifts summer here in very small numbers; breeding was proved in 1995. In this area, there are often sightings of Black Stork, and Griffon and Black Vultures.

Liga para a Protecção da Natureza (see p 140) owns some land in the Castro Verde area and can provide guided visits on request.

# 16 Castro Marim

The Reserva Natural do Sapal de Castro Marim e Vila Real de Santo António (hereafter called Castro Marim) covers an enormous area of wetland, saltmarsh and saltpans at the mouth of the Guadiana. Looking at a map of Iberia, the best way to find Castro Marim is to follow the Guadiana to where it reaches the sea. There it lies, on the western bank, surmounted by two castellated hills which once were islands in a much larger Guadiana estuary. The area has been occupied since Neolithic times; Phoenicians found the site to be fortified and Roman-Lusitanian and Mozarabic remains abound. To the south lies Vila Real de Santo António, once called Santo António de Arenilha, until it was inundated by the sea and rebuilt during the 'reign' of Marquês de Pombal in the 18th century. The whole area has been declared a Nature Reserve. Although not very large, the estuary is very important for breeding, migrating and wintering waterbirds.

*Location*

The site in the far south-eastern corner of Portugal. Full details of the area can be found on the following maps: 1:100,000: 50; 1:50,000: 50-D; 1:25,000: 591 and 600.

*Description*

This ecologically complex area has tidal changes and a fluctuating water table which result in large numbers of fish, molluscs and crustaceans, as well as a wealth of birdlife. The saltmarsh vegetation is rich in species whose life-cycles depend on intermittent winter rainfall.

Close to the River Guadiana and its two minor tributaries (esteiros), the Lezíria and the Carrasqueira, the plant life is characteristic, forming vegetation bands parallel to the water, again much influenced by tidal ebb and flow. Large areas of the drier habitat called 'charcas' are bare of vegetation, saturated with salt and unusual in texture and composition.

*Birds*

The area is close to the north-western coast of Africa and usually enjoys mild winters, and the regular wintering wildfowl and waders may include up to 200 Little Stints, 50 Curlew Sandpipers, as well as hundreds of Black-winged Stilts, Avocets and Black-tailed Godwits. In cold winters the area can hold parties of Black-necked Grebes and many dabbling ducks, as well as Pochard and Coot. Greater Flamingos are found all the year round and can exceed 800 at times with ringed birds commonly seen, most being from the Spanish breeding colonies. Spoonbill numbers fluctuate, and are highest in spring and autumn. Caspian Terns, Little Gulls and marsh terns occur in spring and autumn, the first named roosting on saltpan banks. Little Terns have been seen increasingly in winter and are common summer breeders, while Gull-billed Terns are scarce with odd birds mainly in autumn; Audouin's Gull has turned up in spring and autumn, but Slender-billed Gull remains a major rarity.

Garganey is regular in spring and autumn. Between March and May, Castro Marim holds thousands of migrant waders as well as the large winter populations; Spotted Redshank, Ruff, Little Stint and Curlew Sandpiper can be counted in their hundreds, some in superb summer plumage. Wood Sandpiper and Temminck's Stint are regular. During

Greater Flamingo and Avocet

the breeding season the salt pans hold Kentish Plover, Avocet and Black-winged Stilt. Spring also brings migrating raptors with Montagu's Harrier, Short-toed Eagle, Booted Eagle and Black Kite. A short drive to the hills north of Castro Marim can produce wandering Griffon Vultures at times.

The area boasts at least six breeding larks: Calandra, Thekla, Crested, Wood, Lesser Short-toed and Short-toed; the last named is a summer visitor and passage migrant. Skylarks occur in winter. It is remarkable to watch Short-toed and Lesser Short-toed Larks in the same field of view and note just how different they are in plumage, behaviour and ecological strategy. The race of Lesser Short-toed Lark here is *apetzii*, a dark grey-brown subspecies, which makes identification rather straightforward.

Though Iberian Yellow Wagtail is ubiquitous in summer, three other races – *flava, flavissima* and *thunbergi* -are regular on passage in spring and probably autumn though more difficult to identify at that season. Spectacled Warbler breeds in small numbers in the vegetation along the saltpan edges, arriving in late February and departing in October. Red-necked Nightjar breeds, as well as Melodious Warbler and Woodchat Shrike.

Regular passage migrants include Ortolan Bunting, Pied Flycatcher, Great Spotted Cuckoo (a very early spring migrant), Nightingale, hirundines, warblers, wheatears and Turtle Dove.

*Accommodation*

It is possible to stay at Monte Gordo in reasonably priced hotels or at the camping site there. It is probably better to choose a small Pensão in Vila Real. Many are near the water front and an early morning walk along the seawall to the Ponta de Areia (Banco do O'Brill) can be productive with large numbers of marsh terns common in autumn, as well as gulls, Arctic Skua and occasional Cory's Shearwater.

*Strategy*

The area can be roughly subdivided into three sectors (see map).

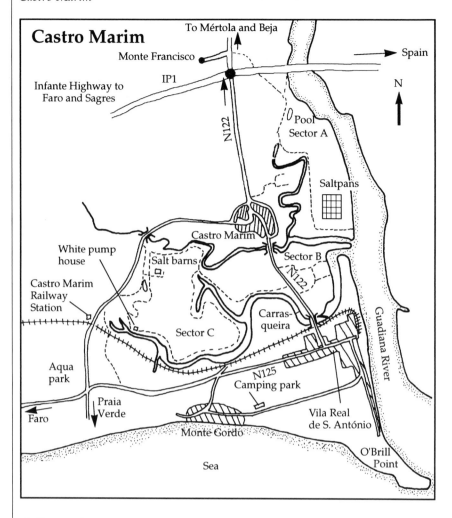

### a) Sector A

This is the area east of the N122, north-east of Castro Marim and consists of saltpans, pasture and some open water pools. The best way to approach it is to enter Castro Marim village and exit north on the road marked 'Espanha'. Almost immediately you can see abandoned saltpans. These are worth exploring taking the first mud track to the right after leaving the village. Walking is preferable here and highly advisable in wet weather. If the pans are wet there can be good numbers of waders and even in winter Little Stint and Curlew Sandpiper are regular. In spring Spectacled Warbler breeds in the thick vegetation and juvenile Lesser Short-toed Larks (wandering from the main breeding site) can be found here in autumn. Return to the main road and continue north; it splits after a while; veer left following the signs saying Monte Francisco and Mértola, otherwise you will end up in Spain!

About 500m further along veer sharply right (opposite Monte Francisco village) along a rough stony track which goes under the main road. This area is good for Black-eared Wheatear in spring and Tawny Pipit in autumn. The track is an excellent route to take in the early morning during spring and autumn. It passes old abandoned saltpans and rough pasture and even in winter should provide Hoopoe, White Stork and Crested Lark. During spring and autumn passage the pools and saltpans can sometimes hold interesting waders like Temminck's Stint and overhead migrants can include Short-toed Lark, Tawny Pipit, Bee-eater and Pallid Swift. After about 1km, the track branches within sight of the Guadiana and it is worth stopping here for a more protracted period. Just in front lie some flooded rushy pools, excellent for waders. In late April the area has held Temminck's Stint, Red-throated Pipit and Grey-headed Wagtail. Just behind these pools lie dry salt pasture, which holds Stone-curlew, Little Bustard, Calandra Lark and Lesser Short-toed Lark throughout the year. At high tide, the extensive saltpans to the right of the track can fill with roosting waders and gulls. The saltpan banks hold breeding Spectacled Warbler in spring/summer. The track to the left leads to the base of the new Infante Bridge, which now links Spain to Portugal. Here Montagu's Harrier can be seen in summer and passerine migrants are very common both in spring and autumn. The track to the right leads through 'charcas' (areas of bare soil) and rough pasture where in spring Lesser Short-toed Lark can be watched closely spinning its extraordinary mimetic song in a Serin-like song flight. Kentish Plover, Black-winged Stilt and Spectacled Warbler all breed here. Stop a little further on and walk into the saltpans along sandy tracks; at high tide this can be extremely profitable, as Gull-billed Tern, Caspian Tern and Audouin's Gull have all turned up here.

**b) Sector B**

   The area south and east from the village of Castro Marim is best reached by driving along the N122 towards Vila Real. Left of the road several tracks run to the river bank (the bank of Carrasqueira). It is advisable to walk these tracks and not to enter the fish farms (easily identified behind high fences). The bird life is similar to that of the previous area, but is less plentiful and is more difficult to observe. Fewer Lesser Short-toed and Calandra Larks occur here, though in spring the site is filled with the crisp clipping notes of Short-toed Larks. Approached in the evening with the sun in the west, superb views can be obtained of Stone-curlew and displaying male Little Bustards. Common species here include Crested Lark, Southern Grey Shrike and White Stork (breeding of the latter may begin in January). In summer, under some meteorological conditions, thousands of swifts feed low over this area on the swirling masses of aerial plankton glinting in the rays of the setting sun – the effect is indescribable.

**c) Sector C**

   This sector lies between the N125, to the south, the N125-6 to the west and north. It is a large area and worth careful, if time-consuming coverage. It can be approached in three ways. The easiest route and one to be taken early in the morning is to leave Vila Real on the N122 and turn left on a short track to where a ruined graffiti covered farmhouse stands beside the Carrasqueira.

Walk westwards with the stream bank to your left and Olive and Carob groves to your right. White Storks breed here in exposed low trees and should not be disturbed. In spring the area can be filled with migrants and usually Black-eared Wheatear can be found near the ruined farmhouse. A host of interesting passerines pass through this site in autumn, many of them trans-saharan migrants. It is worth glancing at the stream occasionally, as Crested Coot, Gull-billed Tern and even Long-tailed Duck have appeared here. The track continues for up to eight winding kilometres round the periphery of the saltpans, but the walk can be very rewarding with close-up views of Greater Flamingo, thousands of waders and Spectacled Warbler singing in spring. In winter Black-necked Grebe can be seen. This track eventually leads to the salt storage area. This is the second entrance gate to the area. It is initially approached by turning left off the Castro Marim-Faro road (N125-6), just after it crosses a metal bridge where Red-rumped Swallow sometimes breeds. Follow this track to the saltworks gate, examining the pools on either side.

Leave your car here outside the gate – you have a choice of two parallel tracks. The inner one (just inside the saltworks entrance) winds its way southwards along saltpan banks where literally thousands of waders and duck can be seen from autumn through to spring. It is best traversed in the afternoon. Rarities, among many interesting migrants, have included Forster's Tern and Wilson's Phalarope. Garganey and Wood Sandpiper are annual. The track ends at the bank of the Carrasqueira near a white pump house. The channel can be filled with wildfowl, though a telescope may be necessary to scan each saltpan bank carefully. If one takes the outer track, it leads to a pool that is often packed with waders and duck when flooded. In summer it only holds breeding Kentish Plover and Spectacled Warbler.

This area (C) has a third point of access reached by driving along the N125 from Faro to Vila Real. About 500m after the turn for Castro Marim, stop at a petrol station on the left and with care negotiate your way along a rough muddy track to some abandoned buildings and an unmanned railway crossing (never, for any species whatsoever, stop on one of these crossings!). This track leads to an old semi-abandoned air strip in rough scrub and pasture. It is an excellent site for Calandra and Lesser Short-toed Larks, Little Bustard and Stone-curlew all year round. Red-necked Nightjar breeds in Maritime Pine on sandy hills nearby and a careful listen at night will reveal singing birds and sometimes breathtaking views of birds feeding on the larger aerial plankton towards dusk.

# 17  Ria Formosa (including Faro)

·  The Ria Formosa is the largest wetland in southern Portugal. It extends for some 60km from Tavira in the east to Ancão in the west and most of this beautiful area is now designated a Natural Park. Human activities are largely traditional. Shellfish collecting is more important here than anywhere else in the country and other activities include fishing and salt production.

The Algarve has a very pleasant climate and continues to be visited, more and more frequently, by package tourists. The successive construction of large tourist complexes and all sorts of infrastructures and facilities has led to the destruction of several wetlands and the Ria Formosa, already peppered with illegal constructions and subject to increased disturbance, has become ever more vulnerable. Nevertheless, 'formosa', meaning beautiful, still applies to this extraordinary place, which holds large numbers of breeding, passage and wintering waterbirds.

*Location*    Ria Formosa is in the Algarve immediately adjacent to Faro. Full details of the area can be found on the following maps: 1:100,000: 53; 1:50,000: 53-A; 1:25,000: 606, 610 and 611

*Description*    Like other coastal wetlands in Portugal, the Ria Formosa is directly connected to the ocean, but there are a low islands and islets between the river mouth and the sea, which form an almost continuous natural chain of dunes and protect the whole area from the destructive force of the sea. In these dunes, the existing vegetation consists mainly of small bushes and a few pine trees.

Salinas (saltpans) are a characteristic feature of most coastal wetlands in Portugal and those in the Ria Formosa are still actively used for salt production. From east to west, small rivers run into the Ria Formosa, forming coastal pools which are important for birds in season. Some of these pools, surrounded with reeds, are of particular interest.

*Birds*    Spring and autumn are the richest seasons in terms of variety of species, while winter is marked by huge concentrations of waterbirds.

Spring migration begins early, with the first hirundines, Yellow Wagtails and Great Spotted Cuckoos being seen in January. However, March and April are the best months to look for migrants and when the wind blows from the east, large numbers of migrants may arrive in the eastern Algarve presumably after crossing the sea or drifting overnight

Subalpine Warbler

from Spain. Redstart, Whinchat, Wheatear and Black-eared Wheatear, Spectacled, Subalpine and Willow Warblers, Golden Oriole and several subspecies of Yellow Wagtail are just a few of the migrants regularly seen in these conditions.

Breeding birds include Purple Heron and Little Bittern. The odd Night Heron, which does not breed any more, still occurs, mainly on passage. The coastal islands, mentioned above, hold a large breeding population of Little Terns, as well as a few Stone-curlews and Short-toed Larks. The Ludo Farm, close to the airport, has breeding Purple Swamp-hens (otherwise occurring only in the reedbeds at Vilamoura and at Quinta do Lago). Other breeding species include White Stork, Collared Pratincole, Woodchat Shrike and Golden Oriole.

Autumn is marked by the variety and abundance of migrant passerines, with Melodious Warblers passing as early as late July; Subalpine and Willow Warblers are seen from mid August onwards, Bonelli's Warbler being seen on occasion. September is the best month for variety and species to be found include Whinchat, Redstart, Bluethroat, Tawny Pipit, Pied Flycatcher, Whitethroat and Grasshopper, Sedge, Reed and Garden Warblers. Waders are also plentiful, with Ringed Plover, Dunlin, Little Stint, Curlew Sandpiper, Ruff, Redshank and Spotted Redshank all common. Birds of prey pass through the area in small numbers, with regular sightings of Red Kite, Booted and Short-toed Eagles and, occasionally, Griffon Vultures. The ETAR waterworks at Montenegro may occasionally hold up to 500 Black Terns, with occasional sightings of the two other marsh terns.

In winter, the area is noteworthy for its huge wintering populations of waterbirds. Ducks can exceed 10,000 and include Wigeon, Shoveler, Pintail, Teal and Pochard, as well as Tufted Duck and Garganey in spring. Wildfowl are best looked for in pools, lagoons and the ETAR waterworks at Montenegro. Several rarities have occurred at these places, including Bean Goose, Long-tailed, Ferruginous, White-headed and Ruddy Ducks. The ETAR waterworks at Montenegro is also a noted haunt of Black-necked Grebe and Little Gull; wintering marsh terns also occur regularly (the three species have overwintered simultaneously on two occasions).

Waders include all the usual wintering species, but there are also a few Black-winged Stilts, Knots and Curlew Sandpipers. Scarce waders have included Temminck's Stint.

Other interesting waterbirds to be found in winter include good numbers of Greater Flamingo, Spoonbill, a few Glossy Ibises and some Caspian Terns, while the passerines include Bluethroat, Reed Bunting, Penduline Tit, Water Pipit and sometimes Goldcrest and Brambling.

*Accommodation*      The Algarve has the highest density of tourist accommodation in Portugal and therefore finding a place to stay should not be a problem, although in mid-summer it is well advisable to book in advance. At Faro and Olhão there are numerous hotels and pensions to suit all pockets. The town of Loulé, lying about 17km to the north-west, also has several good hotels. For those wishing to camp, there is a camping site at Olhão.

*Strategy* This area is good for watching birds at all times of the year, except possibly in June and July because of the heat.

The best sites for birdwatching lie around Faro and can easily be reached by car. To get to the ETAR waterworks at Montenegro, leave Faro westwards on the N125 towards Loulé. Veer left after 3km following the signs to the airport and after 1km take a road to the left signposted Montenegro. Drive onwards, through the next cross-roads, and then southwards, with the airport on your right hand side, until a fence is reached. Veer left and then right, proceed for about 300m until a large lake appears on your left. At this point, park and walk, looking carefully for any birds at the lake. If the sky is clear, the best time to watch here is late afternoon, as the sun will be at your back. A little further ahead there are saltpans and saltmarsh, which are usually good for waders. Waders feed in the muds at low tide and concentrate in the saltpans at high tide, hence try to obtain some idea of the time of high tide.

Ludo Farm is another excellent area. Leave Faro as above but do not veer left to Montenegro, proceed for about 700m further and take a road to the right. This road is in bad condition and after 600m deteriorates into a sandy track. Proceed along this track and you will soon see pines on the left and open fields on the right. A little further ahead, after passing through a gateway, there are saltpans on the left, while on the right hand side there is a meadow, reedbeds and a pool, all of which can be good for wildfowl and for roosting egrets in the evening. This is one of the best sites for Purple Swamp-hen. The

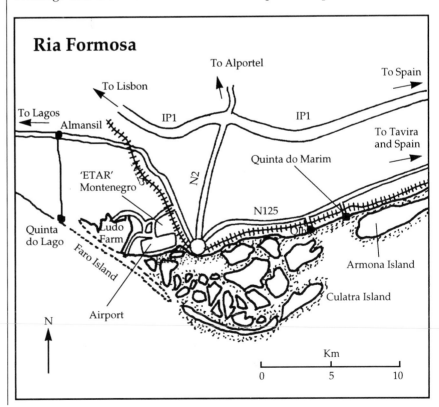

saltpans are good for wintering ducks, Flamingos, Spoonbills, Osprey and Marsh Harrier, as well as for Bee-eater and breeding Little Tern.

Quinta do Lago is a tourist complex with a golf course and few small but important lagoons. The best access is from the village of Almansil. From there follow the signs to Quinta do Lago. On entering the tourist complex (clearly marked) follow the road straight through several roundabouts until the road peters out. Park here and follow the marked 'discovery' trail to the left that passes along the marsh. This leads eventually to the actual lagoon at the edge of the golf course. A small hide has been built there. From this hide Purple Swamp-hen, Little Bittern and a variety of waterfowl can be observed at close quarters. Rarities here have included Crested Coot, White-headed Duck and Marbled Teal.

The headquarters of the Park lie at Quinta do Marim, which is also a good site for watching birds. Leave Faro on the eastern side, towards Olhão. Drive past the town, until a petrol station is reached 2.5km further east. Veer right just before this station, following the road to the headquarters of the Park. The railway line is crossed after 1km (care!) and there is a track to the left after 400m, where a gate marks the entrance of the Quinta do Marim. A small entrance fee is payable. There is a 'Nature discovery track', which is good for watching breeding birds like Dartford Warbler, Woodchat Shrike and Bee-eater, as well as a few other species on passage. There are a few saltpans at the eastern end of the farm, which often hold waders, including Little Stint, Spotted Redshank, Avocet and Black-winged Stilt.

# 18  Sagres and Cape St Vincent

The myth of Sagres as a school of navigation played an important role in European history though much of the history surrounding its importance in Portuguese discoveries has recently been revised. Nevertheless, voyages from Portugal to Africa and Asia, which had begun in the 14th and 15th centuries, were thoroughly organised by the 15th century, aided by instruments acquired from the moorish invaders of North Africa. Sagres, close to Europe's lands-end became a byword in navigation circles, aided in part by King John I's interest and his son's patronage.

From the ornithological point of view today its strategic location makes it an extremely important migration spot, especially in autumn. Because it forms the south-westernmost corner of Europe, unexpected birds can and do appear here. The place has a mystical atmosphere – a happy conjunction of history, geology, climate and wildlife.

*Location*    The headlands at Sagres and Cape St Vincent are situated at the south-west tip of Portugal. Full details of the area can be found on the following maps: 1:100,000: 51; 1:50,000: 51-B; 1:25,000: 601and 609.

*Description*    Cape St Vincent itself is located where the Portuguese southern and western coasts meets. The coastline is mainly formed by rocky seacliffs, with small bays and beaches between. On the western coast, the wind is stronger and the sea can be quite wild, whilst the southern shore is markedly protected from wind and cold.

The whole area is very dry, the landscape being rocky and with low bushy vegetation. Plant species, some endemic and unique not only to Portugal but to the world, can be found here and should not be disturbed or removed. Wheat is the main cereal cultivated, while in uncultivated areas the main activity is sheep grazing, producing a 'downs' effect, not unlike southern England. There are small woods of Maritime Pine dotted about, otherwise the area is treeless. Human presence is marked, with a lighthouse at Cape St Vincent (visible at long range) a light beacon at Sagres within the fortress walls and a harbour village, Sagres itself. Tourism is growing here, but as yet has not disfigured the landscape as has happened further east along the coast.

*Birds*

In autumn large number of migrants concentrate at this corner of Europe. Though much less spectacular than other migration watch points, like the Strait of Gibraltar, the birds are often numerous and certainly most Iberian and west European birds of prey can be seen without difficulty.

Booted Eagle is the most common species and, on good days, one may see 30 or 40 birds; flocks of 400 have been recorded here. Other common species are Black Kite, Honey Buzzard, Short-toed Eagle, Egyptian Vulture and Sparrowhawk. Occasionally, flocks of Griffon Vultures occur, although they are irregular and tend to occur later in the season. Less common species include Red Kite, Lesser Kestrel, Hobby and Eleonora's Falcon, and rarities have included Golden Eagle, Spanish Imperial Eagle and Red-footed Falcon. Bonelli's Eagle and Peregrine occur regularly, although most sightings probably refer to resident birds breeding nearby. Strangely, Black Stork is more regular than White Stork, unlike the situation found at Gibraltar. The Portuguese Society for the study of birds (SPEA) now sponsors annual autumn raptor counts from August to October.

Booted Eagle

Antony S. Disley '97

The migration of passerines is also very interesting and, if weather conditions are favourable, some species may turn up in good numbers, especially in the bushy valleys. The most common species are Nightingale, Redstart, Whitethroat, Garden and Willow Warblers and flycatchers. Less common but still regular are Wryneck, Roller, Rock Thrush, Ring Ouzel, Subalpine and Bonelli's Warblers and Ortolan Bunting. The more open areas often hold migrating Tawny Pipits and several subspecies of Yellow Wagtail as well as Whinchat and Wheatear. Dotterels also occur here at times, being best looked for in uncultivated, dry fields.

Spring migration is markedly weak by comparison, as migrants move through eastern and central Iberia where passage is rapid and purposeful. Many may miss the Algarve altogether. 'Fall' conditions and easterly winds are necessary to see much movement of long range migrants and these conditions may only occur once or twice in an Iberian spring, mainly in April or early May.

Seawatching from Sagres tip and Cape St Vincent (at both lighthouses, respectively) can be good in southerly winds with Cory's and Mediterranean Shearwaters passing in appreciable numbers.

The variety of breeding birds is small, due to the dryness of the area. The most interesting species include Shag, Peregrine, Yellow-legged Gull, Pallid Swift, Thekla Lark, Blue Rock Thrush, Chough and Spectacled Warbler. All these species can easily be found in the area, either on the coastline or in the surrounding open fields.

In winter, there are good numbers of Lapwing, Golden Plover and a few Stone-curlew, while the rocky bluffs just below the lighthouse are a famous spot for finding Alpine Accentor.

*Accommodation*    This area is an acknowledged tourist attraction and accommodation should not be a problem, except possibly in mid summer. At Sagres, there is a wide range of possibilities, from the more simple pensions to expensive hotels. There is also a camping site at Sagres and a pension at Vila do Bispo.

*Strategy*    Sagres can be reached from Faro using the N125 westwards, passing Lagos and Vila do Bispo. From Lisbon, take the A2 southwards to Marateca and then the IP1 until Albufeira in the Algarve. Here follow signs for the N125 westwards as above.

Autumn (August to October) is by far the best time of year to visit the area. At that time of year, the post-breeding migration is at its peak. For soaring birds, it is best to choose a point from where to watch most of the area and wait for the birds to fly over, mainly between 10.00 and 13.00 (this is the time when thermal currents start forming as the temperature rises). One of the best points is located near a pine wood, west of the village of Sagres. To get there, leave Sagres on the N268 that leads westwards to the Cape St Vincent, turning to the right at the curve which lies after the Aldeamentos São Vicente. Continue along a track, which follows a pine hedge (good for passerines at times), turning right at the end and proceeding to the geodetic mark (marked 'Cabranosa' on 1:25000 maps). At Sagres, the passage of birds of prey can either be spectacular or frustrating and the number of birds present

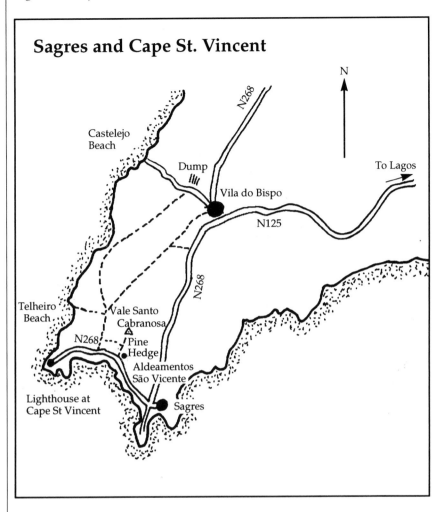

# Sagres and Cape St. Vincent

can change markedly from one day to the other, according to the weather conditions. When the weather is anticyclonic with easterly winds, large numbers of birds of prey concentrate in the area. Ringing has indicated that some of these birds may stay around for several weeks, probably because, unlike Gibraltar, Cape St Vincent truly is land's end. When the wind has a more westerly tendency, raptor passage is minimal.

Apart from the birds of prey, passerines occur, especially in the small hidden valleys close to the coastline or in the pine woods close to the geodetic mark mentioned above. A visit to the beach of Telheiro, which is located about 2 or 3km north of the Cape might also be rewarding, as is the valley called Vale Santo.

Between the Cape itself and the more extensive pine woods to the north, the ground is open and dry and several interesting species can be found. To get there, turn right on the 2nd track after Aldeamentos S. Vicente until a small farm is reached. It is a good spot for Chough, Tawny Pipit and Yellow Wagtail. At Vila do Bispo there is a rubbish dump which sometimes has interesting birds (to reach it follow the road signposted Praia do Castelejo for about 1km).

# ADDITIONAL SITES

Apart from the main sites, which have already been described in detail, Portugal has several other interesting bird areas, many of which have been largely ignored by visiting birdwatchers. In this section, some of these are outlined, together with a short description of the birds to be found there and some hints about exploring the areas (a good road map is essential – see introduction).

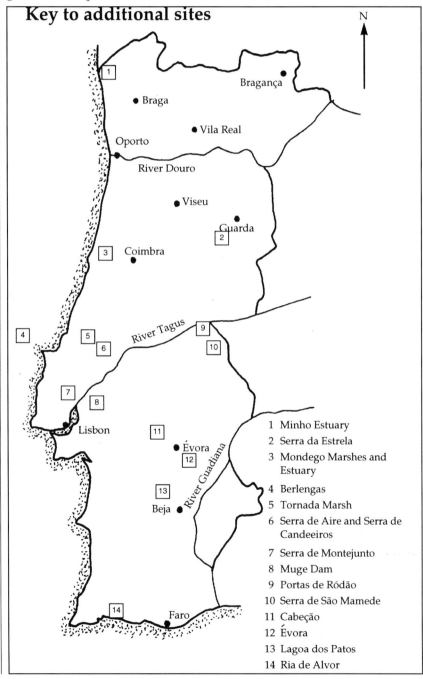

**Key to additional sites**

1 Minho Estuary
2 Serra da Estrela
3 Mondego Marshes and Estuary
4 Berlengas
5 Tornada Marsh
6 Serra de Aire and Serra de Candeeiros
7 Serra de Montejunto
8 Muge Dam
9 Portas de Ródão
10 Serra de São Mamede
11 Cabeção
12 Évora
13 Lagoa dos Patos
14 Ria de Alvor

## Minho Estuary

This small estuary lies in the north-western corner of the country, forming the border with the region of Galicia in Spain. There are some areas of exposed sands, reedbeds and saltmarsh. Breeding species include Kentish Plover, Nightjar, Savi's, Great Reed and Melodious Warblers, Firecrest, Waxbill and Cirl and Rock Buntings.

The surrounding areas consist mainly of open fields with small woods of oak, pine, willow and alder, interspersed with hilly areas. Here, the most interesting species are Scops Owl, Nightjar, Hoopoe, Woodlark, Melodious, Dartford and Sardinian Warblers, Iberian Chiffchaff and Rock and Cirl Buntings. Outside the breeding season, it is possible to find various ducks, waders and gulls in the estuary itself. Seabird movement can be monitored from the mouth of the river and can prove rewarding.

Ferries cross to the Spanish side from Caminha and Vila Nova de Cerveira. To reach the area from Oporto, take the road N13 through Viana do Castelo to Caminha.

## Serra da Estrela

This mountain chain is the highest in mainland Portugal, peaking at 1993m (a 7-metre tower has been built on the top, in order to reach the 2000m mark). It is popular both in summer and in winter as a tourist resort.

In the lower areas (around 1000m) there are sweet chestnut groves, as well as Pine plantations. Above 1300m there are only bushes; the open tops consist largely of bare rock. The scenery is spectacular and many interesting bird species can be found. During a single day in the breeding season, Short-toed Eagle, Montagu's Harrier, Crag Martin, Tawny Pipit, Dipper, Wheatear, Rock Thrush, Firecrest and Rock and Ortolan Buntings can all be seen. A few Black Storks breed in the mountains and Bluethroat has bred recently.

Serra da Estrela lies some 300km away from Lisbon and can be reached via the A1 to Coimbra, then on the IP3 and IP5 to Mangualde and finally on the N232 to Manteigas. This small town can be used as a base for exploration, using the N232 or any of the panoramic roads that lead to the mountainous area. The glacier-carved valley of the River Zêzere, that runs southwards from Manteigas is worth exploring, as are the roads that lead from Covilhã and Sabugueiro to the uplands. Due to the existing tourism facilities at Manteigas, Sabugueiro and Covilhã, finding a place to stay is not a problem, except possibly at critical times such as Carnival, Easter and New Year.

## Portas de Ródão

This site lies close to the border, where the River Tagus enters Portugal. The Portas de Ródão consist of an imposing geological formation which results from the meeting of the River Tagus with the Serra das Talhadas. It takes the form of a narrow passage, the actual Portas do Ródão. The landscape consists mainly of man made terraces, where olive trees are cultivated. Some of these terraces have been abandoned and large areas have become covered with Maritime Pine and Eucalyptus plantations.

Breeding species in this area include White and Black Storks, Black Kite, Griffon Vulture, Bonelli's and Short-toed Eagles, Hobby, Eagle Owl, Bee-eater, Red-rumped Swallow, Crag Martin, Blue Rock Thrush, Black Wheatear, Dartford Warbler, Woodchat Shrike, Golden Oriole, and Rock and Cirl Buntings. The area is also a noted winter haunt of Alpine Accentor. Black Vultures have been seen here occasionally outside the breeding season.

From Lisbon, take the A1 northwards, leave where signs indicate Torres Novas and then proceed eastwards on the IP6 through Abrantes until Vila Velha de Ródão. At Ródão, the cliff on the northern (right) bank is the most convenient from the access point of view. Park near the bridge at Vila Velha de Ródão and walk carefully along the railway line (watch out and listen for approaching trains); look for bird movement on the river, on the opposite slope and on the railway line. It is also possible to drive up the hill to the small medieval tower. This site can be good for raptors, though a long wait may be necessary for the more interesting species.

## Serra de São Mamede

This is an interesting range of hills around the city of Portalegre and the picturesque towns of Castelo de Vide and Marvão. Most of this area is covered by a natural park and habitat is varied, consisting mainly of woodland (Pyrenean Oak, Cork Oak, Maritime Pine, Olive and Sweet Chestnut) and scrubland, consisting mainly of Genista and Sun Rose.

Bird life is varied and over 100 species breed here. Large birds that use thermals for lift thrive here and include White and Black Storks, Black Kite, Egyptian Vulture, Booted and Short-toed Eagles, while Griffon and Black Vultures are often sighted. Bee-eater and Red-necked Nightjar are common, but Roller and Great Spotted Cuckoo are rather localised. Steppe birds are also present, with Little Bustard, Stone Curlew and Calandra and Short-toed Larks. Other passerines include Wood and Thekla Larks, Red-rumped Swallow, Crag Martin, Blue Rock Thrush, Black Wheatear, Melodious, Orphean, Subalpine, Spectacled and Bonelli's Warblers, Woodchat Shrike, Golden Oriole, Spanish and Rock Sparrows, Hawfinch and Rock and Cirl Buntings. Alpine Accentor can be found in mid winter at Marvão castle.

Portalegre can easily be reached from Lisbon following the A1 To Torres Novas, then the IP6 eastwards to Abrantes, the N118 to Alpalhão and finally the IP2 to Portalegre. The park covers most of the area east and north of Portalegre; however the best areas for birdwatching actually lie outside the park, just north of Castelo de Vide. There is a dense network of municipal roads that lead to the villages of Póvoa e Meadas, Beirã and Santo Antonio das Areias, all of which are worth exploring. The castles of Castelo de Vide and Marvão are definitely worth a visit, being scenically attractive and good for birds.

# Mondego Marshes and Estuary

The River Mondego runs from Serra da Estrela, passes through the historic city of Coimbra and enters the sea at Figueira da Foz. Between these two cities, it flows across an area of lowland, with extensive rice fields. The valley holds an interesting bird community and lies conveniently close to Coimbra and to Figueira da Foz. There are several wetlands dotted over the lowland, the main ones being the Arzila, Taipal and Madriz marshes. All these places have a dense growth of aquatic vegetation, especially reeds.

Interesting species to be found in the breeding season are: Purple Heron, Little Bittern, White Stork, Black Kite, Marsh Harrier, Hobby, Cetti's, Reed, Great Reed and Savi's Warblers, Golden Oriole. Wintering species include various ducks, Hen Harrier, Lapwing and Crag Martin, while Red Kite, Bluethroat and Sedge Warbler occur on migration. Squacco Heron (becoming ever scarcer) and Great White Egret have been seen here. The estuary at Figueira da Foz consists mainly of sandflats and intertidal areas, although there are also some saltpans. Black-winged Stilt, Kentish Plover and Iberian Yellow Wagtail breed, while passage brings large flocks of waders and gulls.

Access to the area is as follows: from Coimbra, take the N341, which follows the railway line, along the left bank of the Mondego and proceed for 11km. At Arzila, turn left where the signpost reads Condeixa, Cemitério and Paul, and then to the right following the signs to Paul. This leads to the Arzila Marsh, which has recently been declared a Nature Reserve. To explore the area, follow the marked paths. The Madriz Marsh lies close to Alfarelos and can be reached by proceeding on the N341 from Montemor to Alfarelos, turning left where the signpost reads Soure and continuing along the N342-1, past Casais do Redinho and for another 600m, until a valley with willows and reeds is reached. The marsh lies on the right side of the road. Finally, Taipal Marsh lies close to Montemor-o-Velho and is crossed by the N111, which connects Coimbra to Figueira da Foz. The estuary at Figueira da Foz can be easily reached from the town, crossing the river and turning right where the signpost reads 'Estaleiro' and then again to the right, taking a narrow well surfaced road that leads into the saltpan complex.

# Berlengas Islands

The Berlengas Archipelago lies about 10km off the Portuguese west coast, near Peniche (about 100km north of Lisbon). It is a place of great beauty, with much wildlife of interest. Sadly, nowadays this area is seriously threatened by a mixture of tourism, excessive gull numbers and rats. The Archipelago has been declared a Nature Reserve and consists of one large island, called Berlenga Grande. There are several tiny islets around it, and two further groups of larger islets, a few km away, known as Estelas (the closest one) and Farilhões, respectively. All the islands and islets are very rocky, with steep cliffs dropping almost sheer into the sea. There are no trees, and the vegetation consists mainly of small bushes, some of which are endemic to the archipelago. The only map available is on the scale of 1:5,000 and can be obtained at Instituto Geográfico e Cadastral (see Maps section).

The breeding seabirds are the main attraction of the islands. Guillemot reaches its southern Palearctic limit here but its population has decreased markedly from about 6,000 pairs in 1939 to a handful of pairs presently. These birds belong to the Iberian subspecies, being browner than their northern European counterparts. The islands hold the only population of Cory's Shearwater in mainland Portugal (a few hundred pairs). During the breeding season, at night, the calls of this bird make an impressive sound, echoing through the air like the wail of witches. One of the most remote islets holds the only breeding Madeiran Storm Petrels in mainland Europe. There are about 70 pairs of breeding Shags, forming the most important site for this species in the country. Yellow-legged Gulls are ubiquitous. Seawatching may be rewarding under favourable weather conditions (see under Seabirds).

Apart from the seabirds, the only breeding species are Peregrine and Black Redstart. Other land birds do, however, occur in the islands, especially during migration periods, notably warblers, flycatchers, pipits, wagtails, chats and buntings. Eleonora's Falcon and Red-breasted Flycatcher have occurred.

For one day visits, it is possible to stay at Peniche overnight, taking an early boat (the 'Cabo Avelar Pessoa') across to the island. This boat only runs between mid May and September. For longer stays, It is possible to stay on Berlenga Grande at the camping site. Prospective birdwatchers need to bring their own food, water and bedding. Note that the island has a daily limit of 300 persons so it is advisable to be at the pier at Peniche at least one hour before sailing. From May 15 to June 30 and from September 1 to September 20, the boat departs Peniche at 10.00 and returns at 16.00; during July and August, boats depart Peniche at 09.00, 11.00 and 18.00, returning at 10.00, 16.00 and 18.00. Tickets can be bought ahead about one hour before sailing (telephone 062-782153)

## Tornada Marsh

This small wetland area is located close to the village of Tornada, about 5km to the north of Caldas da Rainha. The region is densely inhabited, land-use is intensive and eutrophication is a problem. The marsh consists mainly of reedbeds, with some areas of open water here and there; the water levels change, according to the rainfall.

Breeding species include Purple Heron, Little Bittern, Black-winged Stilt, Hobby and Savi's, Reed and Great Reed Warblers. In winter, a few wildfowl occur. Other interesting species have put in appearance, like Squacco Heron, Glossy Ibis, Garganey and Wood Sandpiper.

To get to the area from Lisbon, take the A1 motorway exit, leaving it after 45km towards Aveiras de Cima, following the signs to Caldas da Rainha (N366). Leave northwards on the N8 and proceed 5km to Tornada, turning onto the unsurfaced road that passes close to the church at this village. After 200m there is a parking site, from where it is possible to walk to the nearby marsh.

## Serra de Aire and Serra de Candeeiros

These are two ranges of hills, which form the core of a remarkable limestone chain. The whole area is very interesting from the ornithological point of view. The bedrock is mainly calcareous and karst features abound with caves and vertical chimneys. The vegetation consists of scrubland, with Kermes Oak the dominant species. In some areas, there are woods of pine, olive and oak. The landscape is very characteristic, with many stone walls marking the border between the lands belonging to different owners. The area is a Natural Park.

Breeding species include Bonelli's and Short-toed Eagles, Eagle Owl, Chough, Tawny Pipit, Black-eared Wheatear, Bonelli's Warbler, Blue Rock Thrush and Crested Tit. Wallcreeper and Alpine Accentor have been seen here in winter.

It is best approached from Leiria, on the N1 and N243, using Porto de Mós as a base for exploration.

## Serra de Montejunto

This small range of mountains is located about 50km north of Lisbon, rising up to 660m, and is part of the limestone chain of hills running across western Portugal. As the soil is calcareous, there are several deep vertical gorges which hold an interesting community of birds. The vegetation has been largely destroyed by fire in recent years and so most of the area consists of scrubland, with Kermes Oak the most common species. There are also small woods of pine, oak and chestnut.

Breeding birds include Sparrowhawk, Buzzard, Kestrel (which nests in small colonies here), Alpine Swift, Raven and Cirl Bunting. Eagle Owl has been recorded regularly and may be breeding in the area. Other species which have been seen occasionally include Bonelli's Eagle, Peregrine and Alpine Accentor.

The best way to get here is to take the A1 from Lisbon, leaving it at Carregado and proceeding on the N1 until after Ota, where a minor road to the left, indicating Abrigada, leads to the hills.

## Muge Dam

This small wetland lies close to the village of Muge, beside the Tagus, in the province of Ribatejo. It consists of a small dammed area, whose shores are partly covered with vegetation, including some willows. The water body varies according to rainfall and management and in dry years it can drop below ground levels, leaving some areas of exposed mud under those conditions.

Interesting waders may occur, notably Little and Temminck's Stint, Little Ringed Plover (up to 150) and Wood Sandpiper.

In winter the dam is usually full and good numbers of wildfowl can be seen, including Teal and Shoveler. In the willows there is a roost of Cormorants in winter and a heronry (with Cattle and Little Egrets, Night Heron and a few Spoonbills) in summer. In extremely dry years, the marsh is one of the few wet places in the region, thus attracting waterbirds from the surrounding areas.

The area lies close to the Tagus Estuary, from where it can be easily reached. Leave Lisbon on the A1, taking the N10 at Vila Franca de Xira to Porto Alto. From there, take the N118 northwards for 29km, until Muge village is reached. Once in the village, pass the church and turn left where the signs read 'Bombeiros' and 'Junta'. Then, turn immediately right, onto a 'road' called Rua Almirante Reis. Proceed along this unsurfaced road, until the bank of the dam is reached. Walking is essential.

# Cabeção

This is an interesting area lying between the large reservoirs of Montargil and Maranhão, in the province of Alto Alentejo. It consists mainly of Cork Oak groves and has not suffered very much from recent human interference.

Cabeção is well known for its birds of prey, which occur here in fairly high densities. The most common species are Black and Black-shouldered Kites, Buzzard and Booted Eagle. There are also a few pairs of Honey Buzzards, Short-toed Eagles and Eagle Owls. Other breeding birds include White Stork, Bee-eater, Woodlark, Orphean Warbler, Woodchat Shrike, Common Waxbill, Hawfinch and Cirl Bunting. In the more open areas there are a few rice fields, where Cattle Egrets feed, together with Water Pipit in winter. The existing pools are used by various waterfowl in winter. The Maranhão dam is a good place for Crag Martin and Blue Rock Thrush.

To reach the area from Lisbon, take the A1 northwards and exit at Vila Franca de Xira. Proceed on the N10 eastwards, veering left after 26km to Coruche (N119). Beyond Coruche, the N251 runs eastwards through Mora. Finally, the N2 will take you to a crossing where a signpost reads Cabeção. On reaching the village, any of the unsurfaced tracks leading northwards can be used to explore the area. Cabeção can also be reached from Évora in about 30 minutes. Leave Évora northwards on the N370, through Arraiolos and turn right 6km after Pavia.

# Évora

The historic city of Évora lies in the Upper Alentejo and is worth a visit, both for its monuments and for its birds. The surrounding plains are an ocean of wheatland and fallow fields, with a few oak woods here and there.

A range of interesting steppe and open country species can be found and summer visitors include Black Kite, Booted Eagle, Montagu's

Harrier, Black-winged Stilt, Collared Pratincole, Great Spotted Cuckoo, Bee-eater, Roller, Melodious Warbler and Golden Oriole, while resident species include Cattle Egret, Gadwall, Little Bustard, Great Bustard (very scarce), Stone-curlew, Calandra Lark, Azure-winged Magpie and Rock Sparrow. In winter a few Cranes occur in the area, while passage brings interesting waders to the existing small dams.

To visit the plains, take one of the many roads that lead through the area. The small dams are worth visiting; they often hold surprising species. The most interesting ones are:

- Vale de Moura, where waterbirds moult in late summer and which is possibly the best site in the area for Collared Pratincole; to reach Vale de Moura, take the N254 to Alvito and Viana, turning left after 6km, at a pair of pillars, on a track labelled Herdade da Pereira. Proceed for about 1km; permission should be sought at the farm to visit the area. Black Kite, Little Bustard and Calandra Lark occur here.
- Fonte Boa, where Whiskered Terns breed in some years; to get there, take the N254 to Redondo, turning left after 6km to Fonte Boa.
- Divor lies 15km to the north and is reached using municipal roads (look for a sign reading Divor). Interesting birds include Little Bustard, Great Spotted Cuckoo and Rock Sparrow. There is also a dam here which holds some waterfowl.

A large heronry exists near Évora. Look for the N380 (signposted Alcáçovas) that leads south-westwards and drive for about 1km. The colony is on the right side in some pine trees.

## Lagoa dos Patos

A group of two lakes of variable extent, fluctuating markedly in dry winters or when used to flood neighbouring rice fields in summer. They lie just south of a much larger dam, Barragem de Odivelas.

Interesting species in the breeding season include Great Crested Grebe, Grey Heron, Gadwall, Montagu's Harrier, Black-shouldered Kite, Collared Pratincole, Little Ringed Plover, Calandra and Short-toed Larks, Great Spotted Cuckoo and Black-eared Wheatear. In winter, the lake holds thousands of wildfowl, mainly Shoveler, Gadwall and Teal and large numbers of Cormorants. Some Little Bustards occur nearby. Passage species include Gull-billed Tern and marsh terns, Garganey, Black Kite, Blue-headed Wagtail, Tree Pipit, Bee-eater and waders. Rare birds have included Great White Egret and Red-throated Pipit.

Access is relatively straightforward from Ferreira do Alentejo (which lies 20km west of Beja. About 5km east of Ferreira do Alentejo (on the N121) turn left at a signpost reading Cuba. About 3km further on the road passes through Peroguarda village. Look for signs reading Alfundão. In Alfundão, turn left towards Alvito on a poorly surfaced road and about 4km later turn left (westwards) onto a sandy track between wheat fields (the track lies opposite a farm on a slight rise with some Eucalyptus trees).

The best strategy on reaching the lake is to drive around the western end and explore the rice fields. The track continues through a Eucalyptus grove; immediately afterwards turn left. The track winds north westwards towards the Barragem de Odivelas. There is a large heronry of Grey Herons here which should not be disturbed.

## Ria de Alvor

A small estuarine wetland located between Portimão and Lagos, in the Algarve, which holds a variety of habitats, from saltmarsh to bushy areas, together with open fields, pine woods and citrus orchards. Breeding species include Black-winged Stilt, Kentish Plover, Little Tern, Hoopoe, Bee-eater, Red-necked Nightjar, Crested Lark, Melodious Warblers and Woodchat Shrike, while Cattle and Little Egrets breed nearby and usually feed in the area. Passage can be exciting, especially in September and October, as the southern coast of Portugal is a stopping off point for trans-saharan migrants. At that time, it is possible to see many chats, warblers, flycatchers, pipits, swifts and hirundines. Passage of waders is also interesting, with most west European species of wader present in the area, including Curlew Sandpiper, Kentish Plover, Greenshank, Ruff and both godwits. There are also Black Terns on passage and sometimes less common species, such as Audouin's Gull (mainly August). In winter, there are few specialities, but egrets are usually present, Caspian Tern winters in the area, as do several waders and some interesting passerines including Bluethroat, Firecrest, Southern Grey Shrike and sometimes Penduline Tit.

To get there from Faro, take the N125 westwards for about 60km, turning left opposite to a signpost to the right reading Mexilhoeira Grande. By crossing the railway line and following the unsurfaced track for about 3km through almond orchards, the estuarine area can be reached. Park the car and walk.

# Seawatching in Mainland Portugal

Portugal's coastline is 800km long from the mouth of the Minho river in the north-west to the mouth of the Guadiana in the south-east. From a map, it appears eminently suitable for seawatching (see map), but its geographical potential is much reduced by meteorological patterns.

In a typical winter the weather is dominated by an anticyclone lying north of the Azores, bringing dry cool north-east winds. Pelagic seabirds are blown clear of the coast, though wintering Great and Arctic Skuas as well as Razorbills and Mediterranean Gulls may be seen inshore. On average about twice in a month, this weather pattern is modified by frontal systems that bring onshore south-westerly winds, torrential rains and excellent seawatching: Great Skuas, Arctic Skuas, Mediterranean Gull and Little Gull appear, as well as rarer species. If the winds persist, Great Skuas may appear in three figure numbers.

Summer is characterised by the Azores anticyclone with pressure high from May to October; for four to six months, the *nortada* (a northerly airstream) may dominate with clear skies and gusty offshore winds. As a result land-based seawatching may be constantly disappointing, though usually Cory's and Mediterranean Shearwaters, as well as odd skuas may be seen from shore.

Both in spring and in autumn the weather is transitional-cyclonic, though in recent years spring has been dryer and cooler. Frontal weather associated with Atlantic 'lows' does occur and in autumn with onshore winds can produce very good seawatching conditions with hundreds of Storm Petrels, the three larger skuas and Sabine's Gull. However around latitude 40° N, frontal events are short-lived and observations need to be made within twelve hours of the passage of the front. In spring, similar weather may bring heavy passage of Gannets, Great and Arctic Skuas and terns, as well as the ubiquitous Cory's and Mediterranean Shearwaters.

## Breeding seabirds

Cory's Shearwater is a common breeding species in the Berlengas Archipelago. Guillemot has its southernmost breeding site here; the race is *ibericus*. Mainland Europe's only colony of Madeiran Storm Petrel lies also in the surrounding islets. Access is prohibited but birds can be heard at night over Berlenga Grande during the breeding season. Kittiwake has bred.

Yellow-legged Gull and Shag also breed along the coast south from Peniche.

## Pelagic observations

Despite some exciting seawatching from land in recent years, the predominance of the offshore winds in Portugal as mentioned above mean that seabirds are actually best observed from a boat. Fortunately, the same offshore winds are largely responsible for a remarkable upwelling of cold enriched water along the 200m bathymetric contour where the continental shelf slopes abruptly to 1000m. This bathymetric contour line runs relatively close to the Portuguese coast and can be easily reached by boat in a few hours. From July to September, Wilson's Storm Petrels are very regular in small numbers and skuas, including Long-tailed Skua, have been observed closely. Sabine's Gull are seen annually and of course Cory's, Great and Sooty Shearwaters are guaranteed. Over a thousand Storm Petrels have been seen together and moulting Mediterranean Shearwaters are always present in July and August. In recent years, pelagic transects between Portuguese and Macaronesian waters have revealed that Bulwer's Petrel and Little Shearwater are clearly regular to within 90km of the Portuguese coast. White-faced Storm Petrel occurs annually, especially in the region of the Gorringe bank, which lies about 250km south-west of Cape Saint Vincent, and both Red-billed Tropicbird and Fea's Petrel have been observed within 300km of the Portuguese coastline.

For pelagic trips it is best to dose oneself the night before with pills, take a water proof and arrange to have about 15 gallons of chum aboard (a mix of sardines and oil). Autumn is considerably better than spring for passage migrants at sea.

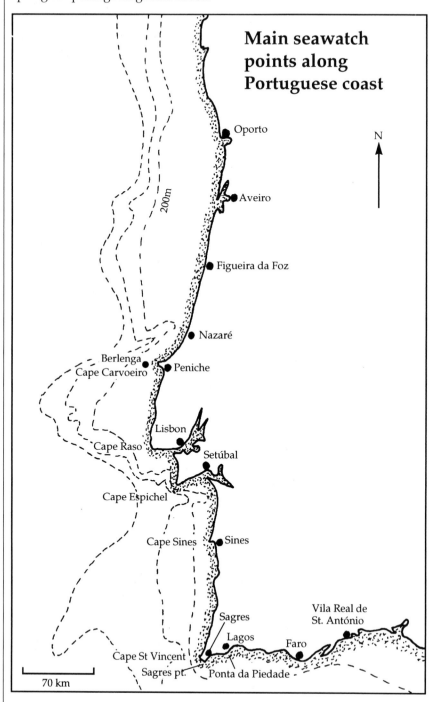

**Main seawatch points along Portuguese coast**

N

200m

- Oporto
- Aveiro
- Figueira da Foz
- Nazaré
- Berlenga
- Cape Carvoeiro
- Peniche
- Lisbon
- Cape Raso
- Setúbal
- Cape Espichel
- Cape Sines
- Sines
- Vila Real de St. António
- Sagres
- Lagos
- Faro
- Cape St Vincent
- Sagres pt.
- Ponta da Piedade

70 km

# Seawatching and 'pelagics'

## a) Algarve

Headlands here are worth visiting, though only in SE to SW (occasionally NW) winds are the scarcer species likely to be seen.

Ponta da Piedade: lies about 1.5km south-west of Lagos. There is a lighthouse here and good cover for passerine migrants also. The bus from Lagos to Vila do Bispo and Sagres passes close by.

Sagres / Cape Saint Vincent: From Faro buses run daily (changing at Lagos) and from Lisbon buses run twice a day, also changing at Lagos. Access by car is straightforward (see Sagres / Cape St Vincent section).

Seawatching at Sagres is best under cloudy skies and SE to SW winds. The best site at Sagres is at the lightbeacon behind the 'fortaleza' walls. Watch out for seabirds passing very close, which fly almost beneath an observer at times. Seawatching has been carried out off Cape St Vincent and the results may warrant further study. The grounds of the lighthouse are protected against the elements but are very high. It is very dangerous to try to descend further because of the scree on the slopes of the cliff.

There are several skippers at Sagres harbour specialising in deep sea angling for tourists. 'Francisco' runs an excellent service and can be contacted through the hotels (see the notice boards in the lobby). He may reduce costs for parties of non-fishermen and will willingly steer any special course required. Usually these trips last all day. Off Sagres, the best area (at least in autumn) is the 95m depth contour. Chum can be requested before hand.

In autumn, the three large skuas and Sabine's Gull can certainly be seen and Wilson's Storm Petrels appear sometimes in moderate numbers and well within camera range. Cory's and Mediterranean Shearwaters are guaranteed. This area, the western approaches to the Gulf of Cadiz is very rich at times and its proximity to Macaronesian waters and the African coast makes any seatrip exciting.

## b) Sines

For all west coast sites, the best conditions are westerly or NW winds. Remember evening seawatching can be difficult in sunny conditions anywhere along the west coast.

Sines point lies just north of the oil terminal and the fishing harbour and can be reached within two hours from Lisbon by taking the road south to Setúbal, and following the signs for Tróia and Ferryboat. The point itself is best located by looking for the small lighthouse immediately inland from the point. The site is low-lying, but surprisingly good. A visit can be combined with birdwatching at Santo André Lagoon.

In westerly winds or even flat calm conditions, terns and petrels are regular. Sabine's Gull, and Wilson's Storm Petrel have been seen just offshore. Cory's and Mediterranean Shearwaters are guaranteed from March to October.

## c) Cape Espichel

The 200m underwater contour lies close inshore and the cape itself may prove interesting but needs more study. About 750m to the NE of the lighthouse there is an alternative site that lies at the end of a track (2nd on left on leaving the Cape) that leads to the sea. Seawatching can be carried out from the fossil sand-dunes. There are several converted skiffs that run sea trips from Setúbal to Cape Espichel and back. The most reliable is the 'Riquitum' which can be found at the 'Tropical' restaurant close to the car ferry terminal. Ask for João Barbas. An alternative is to ask for the 'Noël', a fishing trawler docked at Doca das Fontainhas (also in Setúbal) and speak to Senhor Rui. Chum can be arranged.

Cory's and Mediterranean Shearwaters are common and passage of terns may be interesting. Little Shearwaters and Wilson's Storm Petrel have been seen just offshore and the large submarine canyon to the south of the head is worth traversing, as it creates local upwelling conditions in late summer and winter.

### d) Cape Raso

This seawatch point lies west of Cascais, about 25km west of Lisbon and is easily reached by car or bus. Take the signs that indicate Boca do Inferno and continue until a red coloured metal lighthouse appears. Here you can seawatch from your car (park very carefully, well off the road) or request permission from the lightkeeper to use the added height of the lighthouse storeroom. Cape da Roca some km further north, is too high for effective seawatching, despite being the most westerly point in continental Europe.

### e) Cape Carvoeiro (Peniche)

Peniche lies 100km north of Lisbon and can be reached in two hours by car from Lisbon. Follow the A8 motorway that leads to Torres Vedras and then follow signs for Peniche.

In Peniche itself follow the signs reading 'Cabo Carvoeiro'. The best sites are just north of the lighthouse or in a secluded cleft of rocks to the left of the Café, near the lighthouse. Use the stone stairs and be very careful.

There is a regular passenger ferry from mid May to September from Peniche to Berlenga island. Interesting seabirds are often seen on this journey. It is best to take an early ferry (09.00 hours) and return on a late crossing (18.00 hours). Alternatively, contact 'Turpesca' in Peniche (tel. 062-789960), and ask for Senhor Bernardo. Costs may be reduced for non-fishermen. The best sites lie just west and north of the Farilhões, a group of islands north-west of Berlenga island itself. Chum can be arranged in advance. Several of the fishermen will take passengers and sometimes will rent out their boat for the day. When arriving at the quay, ask for Senhor Gomes.

Though most unlikely to be seen at sea, Madeiran Storm Petrel breeds in the Berlenga archipelago. Wilson's Storm Petrels are regular from June to October and all four skuas have been seen in autumn (from the middle of August onwards), especially from ship board.

Cory's and Mediterranean Shearwaters are guaranteed, Leach's Storm Petrel, Storm Petrel and an interesting set of terns and gulls can also be seen on autumn passage both from land and from a boat. In winter, Leach's Storm Petrel, Grey Phalarope and Little Auk have been seen. The passage of Razorbills, Gannets and Common Scoters can be spectacular.

### f) Ria de Aveiro

In the first hours of daylight, when birds are most mobile and the light is favourable the best seawatching sites are at São Jacinto and at Barra pier. Though the former is better located in terms of seawatching, access difficulties often makes the latter an easier option. To reach Barra pier from Aveiro, use the EN109-7.

During the remainder of the day bird movement is much reduced though the area immediately west of the northern sandbar off São Jacinto is often used by seabirds for roosting and feeding due to its unparalleled shallowness.

Outside the breeding season, it is possible to find Cory's and Mediterranean Shearwaters, Yellow-legged Gulls, Common Scoters (about 4000) and Red-throated Divers.

# MADEIRA

The Archipelago of Madeira was discovered about 600 years ago, when Portugal led Europe in navigational skills and dangerous journeys. It lies about 800km south of Lisbon and about 350km west of the North-west African coast; the main island is bisected by longitude 17° west.

Often called the 'Pearl of the Atlantic', the autonomous territory of Madeira actually consists of two main islands (Madeira and Porto Santo) and two clusters of smaller islands, Ilhas Desertas and Ilhas Selvagens respectively. Famed for its seabirds, many of which it shares in common with other Macaronesian sites, like the Canary Islands, it also has an interesting suite of subspecies and a unique pigeon species.

## Travelling to Madeira

Though liners still call at Funchal, the capital and main port, most visitors arrive by plane. There are regular flights and charters available from most European cities and it is worth consulting teletext to secure cheap last minute seats (flight time from Gatwick is 4 hours).

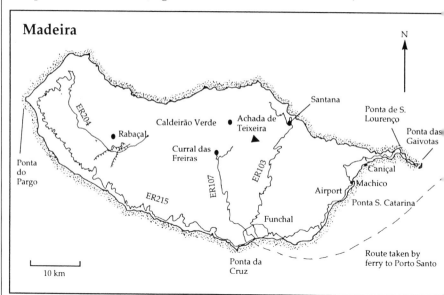

## Travelling in the archipelago

The public transport system on Madeira island is efficient and on a visit to the tourism office or hotels on the Avenida Arriaga one can stock up on maps, bus timetables and brochures advertising boat trips. If planning to explore the island, taxis are available but costs must be carefully calculated and written down before setting out. Car-hire costs are higher than than average European rates but apart from the main companies represented at the airport and in Funchal, smaller companies are open to negotiation. It may be impossible to hire a car in early August.

Apart from the road system, hydrographic studies have identified over 200 water ways flowing into over 100 river basins. These have been canalised to irrigate the terraces that so characterise the Madeiran landscape. The channels are cut-away water courses only a few metres wide and alongside these 'levadas', some of which tunnel through mountains, are narrow pathways (rights of way). By following these paths, one can explore many kilometres of strange and mysterious byways, luxuriant with flowers and birds. The best map to use is the Clyde leisure maps which clearly indicate these routes (scale 1:70.000).

## Porto Santo

There are three ways of getting to Porto Santo. There are daily flights from Funchal which can be arranged at the TAP offices on Avenida do Mar, Funchal. There is a daily ferry (The 'Lobo Marinho', costing about 9500 Esc. return) which crosses from Funchal to Porto Santo in two and a half hours. Any travel agency can arrange this though it is better to personally organise the tickets, especially in summer, at the Marina (Doca Nova). A slower alternative is the n/m Madeirense, a small cargo boat which takes about four hours to reach Porto Santo from Funchal and requires an overnight stay except on Fridays (costs about 7000 Esc. return). It sails from Funchal at 08.00 hrs and returns at 19.00 hrs (on Fridays it leaves Funchal at 17.00 hrs and only stops long enough at Porto Santo to pick up passengers). Details can be obtained on board or at dock-side opposite the Doca Nova. Once on Porto Santo, transport is limited and it may prove very difficult to hire cars. Motor scooters ('motos') are sometimes available.

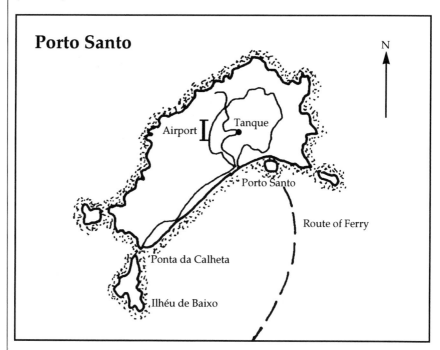

## Desertas and Selvagens

During the summer months, there are sometimes limited landing rights on Deserta Grande and Ilhéu Chão for certain nominated craft. Arrangements can be made at the marina for sailing trips close to the islands: there are at least five game fishing companies to choose from as well as the larger 'Costa do Sol' enterprise (Doca da Marina phone 091-224390). The Madeiran Natural Parque headquarters at Caminho do Meio, 9000 Funchal, will also supply information on access to the Desertas.

Legitimate scientific research and proper authorisation from the Instituto de Conservação da Natureza at Rua Ivens, Funchal or Rua Filipe Folque, 46, 1000 Lisboa, are necessary to visit the Selvagens islands. Permission from the Portuguese Naval authorities is also needed to land on the Selvagens.

## Accommodation

Ranges from the super deluxe hotels of south coast Madeira to small pensions and clearly there are advantages to both. When booking try to locate 'your' hotel on a map of Madeira. This can have a major bearing on the success of your trip especially if you intend to seawatch, as some south coast hotels overlook the sea and one can seawatch from the comfort of the balcony of the hotel grounds.

An average 'pensão' in Funchal will cost about £15 per night. Though there are many hotels scattered along the south coast it may prove difficult to find accommodation during the summer months or at Christmas. Advance booking through a travel agency is advisable.

Accomodation in Porto Santo can sometimes be arranged through travel agencies in Funchal (Av. M. Arriaga). Accomodation on Ilhas Desertas and Ilhas Selvagens is only available to those undertaking long term scientific studies.

## Food and Drink

Food and wine are excellent and local special dishes should be tried. However, be extra careful about combining alcohol with driving as maniacal drivers abound in Madeira and quite correctly the law is very strict about blood alcohol levels.

As is the case of Continental Portugal, tapwater is drinkable but local mineral waters in bottles are a more pleasant alternative. Medical facilities are concentrated in Funchal, but for the occasional diarrhoea episode common to most holidays, bring Imodium tablets. These are also available in local pharmacies.

## Description

The remarkable landscape of Madeira, with its dark rocky vistas, extinct volcanoes, precipitous ravines and misty heights has been moulded and remoulded by tectonic events. On Madeira itself the land slopes markedly upwards from a sheltered southern shore to an east-west backbone of rugged peaks and staggering cliffs.

The climate in the archipelago varies from subtropical superhumid to subhumid dry and is dominated by the NE trade winds off Africa, about 500km to the East. On Madeira island (65km long by 25km wide) these climatic conditions are much altered by rapid changes in relief. Together with man's intervention this produces a south-north zonation from southern shore banana plantations, through characteristics terraced small-holdings to subtropical laurel forest, constantly swathed in rolling mist.

Porto Santo island, lying to the north and east of Madeira itself is a smaller island, within sight of Ponta de São Lourenço at the eastern end of Madeira and like that area, has a much drier climate. A spectacular sandy beach stretches along the south coast for about 10km. The vegetation is relatively sparse and concentrated into a few areas outside Vila Baleeira, the largest town.

South and slightly east of Madeira lie the Desertas Islands (Ilhéu Chão, Deserta Grande and Bugio) centred around 32°30′N, 16°30′ W and rising to 478m on Deserta Grande. They are visible from Madeira and appear tantalisingly close but are difficult of access and zealously protected by the Natural Park authorities.

About 160km southwards, out of sight of Madeira (basically 30°N, 16°W), lie the Ilhas Selvagens (Selvagem Grande and Selvagem Pequena). These are dry volcanic islands fully thanks to the Natural Park authorities and the Zino family; they hold a global patrimony of biodiversity.

**When to go** Seabirds and endemica apart, trans-saharan migrants are best seen in April and September but like all islands Madeira may turn up all kinds of vagrants and its position off the African coast only adds to the excitement of finding the unexpected. June to September is best for seabirds.

**Birds** Madeira is probably best known for its seabirds but the endemic land birds, both species and subspecies, are of considerable interest and importance. It is worth remembering that the Laurel forest occupies an eighth of Madeira island, the largest area of this type of habitat left in the world.

For birdwatchers brought up in Continental Europe, the seabirds of the Macaronesian archipelagos have a quality almost beyond words.

Long-toed Pigeon

ASD 97

Their names carry a charisma often being called after the remote islands on which they breed or after early naturalists who explored this area. The inventory is astounding, including as it does species like Bulwer's Petrel (c. 3500 breeding pairs), Madeiran Storm Petrel (c. 2500 breeding pairs) and Fea's Petrel (c. 120 breeding pairs).

There are special species and subspecies endemic to the Macaronesian area to be found among the land birds; Madeira/Porto Santo can boast three at least – Berthelot's Pipit, Plain Swift and Canary.

More closely associated with Madeira's Laurel forest are Long-toed Pigeon (found nowhere else in the world) as well as Madeiran Sparrowhawk (race *granti*), Madeiran Firecrest (race *madeirensis*), Madeiran Chaffinch (race *madeirensis*) and the beautiful Madeiran Spectacled Warbler (race *bella*).

Spanish Sparrows were introduced this century and are common in both rural and urban settings; Rock Sparrows (race *madeirensis*) occur in the drier east of the island. Finally, non-migratory Blackcaps (race *heineken*) might seem an overrated species, ubiquitous, mellifluous and highly variable. However, in the absence of competitors they have evolved to occupy a wide range of insectivorous niches and their very variability makes for fascinating observations.

## Some suggested itineraries

### a) From Funchal eastwards to Ponta de S. Lourenço

Beginning at Funchal, it can be rewarding to walk the high black wall along the outer harbour. Gulls and Terns roost here, including Yellow-legged Gulls (race *atlantis*), Common Terns and sometimes Roseate Terns. The walk from Avenida do Mar to the outer wall passes over the Ribeira de S. João (now being sanitised); Nearctic waders and gulls have been seen there. An early morning or late afternoon seawatch from the wall can be rewarding with a predominantly westwards movement in the morning and marked eastwards movement in the evening. Cory's are ubiquitous but sometimes Bulwer's Petrel and Little Shearwaters can be seen at moderate range in substantial numbers. Plain Swifts roost just west of the wall.

The best route eastwards out of Funchal passes the airport (ER101). Along the route between Funchal and the airport, Plain Swifts can be seen scything at breakneck speed along the overhangs (do not became distracted, as local drivers tend to mimic the swifts).

At the airport, the small pebbly beaches there can hold small numbers of interesting waders and the headland at Ponta de Santa Catarina can be occasionally good for evening sea-watching in windless conditions. Pallid Swifts occur here in summer.

Just beyond the airport is an area of hotels and restaurants but the bay at Machico is still good for terns and gulls. Because of the persistent northerly winds it can be very difficult to seawatch from here eastwards but with a telescope turned on Bugio (the outernmost island in the Desertas), the extraordinary gad-fly action of Fea's/Zino's Petrel can occasionally be seen, normally at very long range. Here also Spanish Sparrows begins to increase and Canaries can often be seen and heard.

Buzzard and Kestrel are extremely common along this route. Beyond the village of Caniçal where the island race of Spectacled Warbler is regular, the dusty road climbs to a car park from where it is possible to walk eastwards in a 'desert-scape' for about another kilometre (the actual Ponta de São Lourenço cannot be reached by land). Rock Sparrows and Berthelot's Pipits abound here and a myriad of grounded trans-Saharian birds can occasionally be seen. At night the air may be filled with the sounds of Cory's Shearwater, but seawatching from here or at Ponta das Gaivotas nearby is consistently disappointing.

### b) North from Funchal to Santana

Take the ER103 north following signs for Monte until Monte and the Poiso cross-roads are reached at 1.400m above sea level. The woods in this area hold two Madeiran subspecies of interest, Firecrest and Chaffinch. Their calls are distinctly different to those of their continental counterparts, and the latter species has much of its pink coloration suppressed.

Past Poiso, with signposts reading Ribeiro Frio, the road descends into a long deep laurel filled valley. Early in the morning, it is worth stopping at the lay-bys here and watching the tree line. This is an excellent site for seeing Laurel Pigeons and Woodcock, as well as Sparrowhawk and Buzzard though clouds and mist may obscure views at times. Proceeding a little further, signs for Trout Hatchery appear on the right side of road. Locate a café called 'Victors'. Park here and, crossing the road, follow a trail marked Balcões which parallels a levada. A strategic fork on this path should be followed northwards for a short distance. The trail now swings south and then south-westwards until Balcões is reached. The breathtaking views over the Laurel forest make the 20 minutes walk worthwhile and patience is all that is needed to find Laurel Pigeons, their tail markings unique even in the dim mist. The ER103 intersects with the ER101 at Faial on the north coast. Turn left towards Santana and after about 9km, turn left onto the ER101-3 near a garage following signs for Achada do Teixeira and Casa das Queimadas. About 9km onwards, there is a good parking and picnic site in the forest park at Pico das Pedras. A levada runs west from here to Caldeirão Verde. This is one of the most regular sites in Madeira for seeing Laurel Pigeon at close range and both Chaffinch and Firecrest are often seen here.

### c) Funchal to Curral das Freiras

Take the ER203 from the western end of Funchal town following signs for Curral das Freiras. The road winds its way upwards through banana and sugar cane groves past levadas, ravinas full of tall cane and trellised vines to almost $1^1/_2$ km above the sea. Paths lead north from here towards Pico das Torrinhas and Pico Ruivo. Beware of getting lost in frequent mist.

The entire mountain has an ethereal quality and perhaps it is not surprising that the last Zino's Petrel breeds somewhere in these astounding mountains (clearly no further details can be given). At this altitude, Firecrests, Chaffinches and Plain Swifts can be seen and Buzzard is common. Sometimes Woodcock can be found.

### d) Funchal west to Porto da Cruz

Take the ER101 west from Funchal (using public transport or car). The route is scenic and can be walked (3km) with good views of Plain Swift, sometimes Pallid Swift and ubiquitous Grey Wagtails and Island Canaries.

At Porto da Cruz, the grounds of the Carlton Palm's Hotel or just outside it form an excellent base for seawatching (it is the most southerly point on Madeira and is consistently good compared with sites like Ponta das Gaivotas at the eastern end of Madeira and Porto Moniz on the north-west coast).

Observations from here reveal a regular movement westwards in the morning and eastwards in the evening (presumably as birds return to the breeding sites at Ponta de São Lourenço and the Desertas).

Similar to observations from Funchal harbour, the birds tend to follow lines parallel to the coast and apart from the ubiquitous Cory's Shearwater, Bulwer's Petrel and Little Shearwater are regular, sometimes common, Madeiran Storm Petrel occasionally occurs inshore and Zino's/Fea's Petrel has been seen sometimes flying eastwards here within 250m of the shore. White-faced Storm Petrel has also been reported from this potentially excellent headland.

### e) Funchal west to Rabaçal via ER101 and ER204

This is a long tortuous route to the far western end of Madeira leaving Funchal on the ER101 westwards. Ponta do Pargo can often be good for seabirds towards evening and the fork eastwards brings one along the ER204 to Rabaçal. Here several 'levadas' run north-south and are worth walking – Long-toed Pigeon, Madeiran Chaffinch and Woodcock can all be seen.

### f) Porto Santo town west to Ponta da Calheta

Assuming that one has arrived by boat, the best strategy is to walk from the town westwards to Ponta da Calheta, the westernmost point on the island (a walk of about 6km). Hoopoe, Plain Swift, Spectacled Warbler, Spanish Sparrow and Canary are common. The 500 m wide strait called Boqueirão de Baixo, between Ponta Calheta and the Ilhéu de Baixo, is worth watching at dawn as Bulwer's Petrels and Little Shearwaters leave to feed offshore (remember that in winter Bulwer's Petrel may be absent and Fea's/Zino's Petrel difficult to find).

There are three small water bodies on Porto Santo, at the foot of Pico de Ana Ferreira, at Lapeiras and the appropriately named Tanque, quite close to Porto Santo itself. Nearctic waders have been seen here and altogether Porto Santo has all the makings of an excellent bird observatory, even if access and accommodation are costly.

### g) Maritime routes

To approach seabirds more closely boats are necessary. There are several possibilities:

– at least one Funchal-based yacht, the 'Albatroz' sails east and west along the south coast. It can be booked at the Marina though sailing times are erratic to say least.

– several game fishing companies have offices at the Marina (Doca

Nova) and for birdwatchers there is usually a reduced fee. These travel closer to the Desertas and can provide excellent opportunities to see and photograph seabirds at close range. However, these boats are small buoyant craft and roll heavily in even the highest swell. Negociate prices before sailing and dose one-self with travel-sickness pills.

– a small cargo boat, the n/m Madeirense plies between Funchal and Porto Santo, taking about four hours to do so. Views from the bow of this boat can be outstanding especially for photography in calm conditions but it is much safer to stand close to the bridge and regularly watch through 180°. The only drawback is that the boats schedule requires an overnight stay on Porto Santo island except on Fridays. Details can be obtained on board or at the dockside opposite the Doca Nova (return fare about 7000 Esc.).

– the fourth alternative and probably the most reliable and regularly successful is the Porto Santo ferry ('Lobo Marinho'). There are daily sailings at 8.00 from Funchal (Doca Nova). It leaves Porto Santo 11 hours later (on Friday it departs Funchal 17.00 hrs and only stops long enough at Porto Santo to pick up passengers). The voyage takes about 2 hours and with luck (and permission) one can stand close to the bridge during the voyage. Work hard to get this privilege. It is well worth it. Typically from Funchal to opposite Santa Cruz, Cory's Shearwater and Common Terns are everywhere and as the boat bears north-eastwards to sail between the Ponta de S. Lourenço light house and Ilhéu Chão (Desertas), hundreds of Little Shearwaters and Bulwer's Petrels can often be seen. Usually between 5 and 25 Fea's/Zino's Petrels can be seen here, passing obliquely across the waves, looking like some odd combination of giant Little Gull and Pratincole. Though there are two species breeding in these waters, they have so far proved impossible to separate at sea. So few Zino's Petrels (*Pterodroma madeira*) actually exist (they breed only in upland Madeira) that most observations at sea are probably of Fea's Petrel which breeds on the Desertas.

Nearer Porto Santo, Little Shearwaters and Bulwer's Petrels may still be abundant especially towards dusk. During migration periods, all four skuas species have been seen here.

# Selective Species List for Mainland Portugal

**Cory's Shearwater.** It breeds only in the Berlengas archipelago, where it is common, mainly from May to August. It can be found however from late March onwards along the entire coast, best seen from prominent capes, like Cape Raso and Cape St Vincent.

**Madeiran Storm Petrel.** A very scarce breeding species in the Berlengas archipelago, first found in 1980 on one of the outer islets. It has also been heard singing over Berlenga Grande itself at night. As elsewhere, its breeding biology and population size are relatively unknown. This nucleus of birds forms the only breeding population of this species in continental Europe, but, like other petrels, can be very difficult to find due to its nocturnal habits.

**Little Bittern.** A scarce summer visitor to most reedbed areas and to dense riparian cover. Not always easy to observe. Places to look for it are Boquilobo Marsh, Sado Estuary (especially Murta Dam), Tornada Marsh and Santo André Lagoon, although it is known from a variety of other sites in central and southern Portugal. The 'song' is distinctive and dawn and dusk are the optimum times to search for the species.

**Black-crowned Night Heron.** This migrant heron has a very localised distribution in Portugal. There is a large colony at Boquilobo Marsh and another at Muge Dam. Odd individuals turn up at other sites.

**Squacco Heron.** A heron of uncertain status, which has certainly bred regularly at Boquilobo Marsh in very small numbers and more recently at Murta Dam. Sightings are occasionally made at other sites throughout the year.

**Purple Heron.** A summer visitor to most wetlands in the country, where it is locally common and may form loose colonies in large reedbeds. More numerous in coastal areas, such as the Tagus and Sado estuaries, it breeds also in certain inland sites, like Boquilobo Marsh.

**Black Stork.** A rare breeding species, restricted to relatively undisturbed, mostly uninhabited inland areas. The important sites are at International Tagus and at International Douro. Breeds locally at Montesinho, in the Guadiana valley and around Barrancos. During migration, it can be seen occasionally in coastal areas, most regularly at Cape Saint Vincent in autumn. Odd birds may winter in the south.

**Glossy Ibis.** Scarce, but increasingly regularly recorded in small numbers in wetland areas, such as Santo André Lagoon, mostly outside the breeding season.

**Spoonbill.** Mainly a passage migrant, which can occur in any wetland area, although it is usually most numerous at Castro Marim, where over 100 birds are regularly seen. In 1988, this bird was found breeding in Portugal for the first time, at Boquilobo Marsh, and since then has been found breeding at three other sites. Do not disturb the birds at these sites. Some birds seen outside the breeding season are of Dutch origin (based on colour rings).

**Greater Flamingo.** Does not breed, but is usually present throughout the year in the Tagus, Sado, Ria Formosa and Castro Marim areas, with over 2000 birds at certain times of the year, especially in autumn. There has been a very marked increase in recent years.

**Red-crested Pochard.** The species breeds regularly only at Santo André Lagoon and then only in very small numbers. However, in some years over 1% of the world's population winters in Portugal, mainly in the south. Ringing returns suggest that most are of Spanish origin.

**Black-shouldered Kite.** This resident species has increased in recent years and is widely distributed over most of southern and eastern Portugal. It is fairly common in the province of Alentejo and is easy to observe in the Tagus Estuary and at Mourão.

**Red Kite.** A decreasing breeding species, nowadays restricted to the more remote inland areas close to the Spanish border, like Barrancos, International Tagus and International Douro. More numerous in winter, but still largely restricted to the easternmost areas. Migrants occur on coastal sites.

**Egyptian Vulture.** As a summer visitor it breeds in the eastern part of the country, but is usually scarce, except at International Douro, where it is one of the most common soaring birds. It can also be found at the International Tagus. Occurs regularly on autumn migration at south-western watch points.

**Griffon Vulture.** Locally common in undisturbed inland areas, where it can be seen in small flocks. The largest numbers can be seen in the International Tagus and International Douro valleys and it is also seen regularly at Barrancos. Very scarce elsewhere, although it occurs regularly on autumn migration at Cape Saint Vincent.

**Black Vulture.** Usually seen in very small numbers, most often singly among flocks of Griffon Vultures. Occurs mainly in the International Tagus, Barrancos and Mértola, with exceptional reports from other sites; breeding attempts were reported in 1996.

**Short-toed Eagle.** A widespread summer visitor (as Booted) arriving in March, found over most of the country but most abundantly in the south. Tagus Estuary, Gerês and Cabeção are good sites for this species. Birds on passage occur at Cape Saint Vincent.

**Spanish Imperial Eagle.** A rare bird, it is recorded almost every year in Portugal, but its breeding status is uncertain. Young birds can turn up almost anywhere.

**Booted Eagle.** A widespread summer visitor, it occurs mainly in the southern half of the country, where it can be locally common. Possibly the best region to locate the species is the Alentejo, especially in open Cork Oak areas. Numerous in autumn in the Sagres area. Booted Eagles overwinter in very small numbers in southern coastal Portugal.

**Bonelli's Eagle.** An uncommon resident species with a very localised distribution. Occurs mostly in remote areas and in very small numbers. Regularly sighted at International Douro, International Tagus and Arrábida, among other places.

**Lesser Kestrel.** As is the case in many European countries, the species has declined sharply in the last twenty years, and is nowadays a very rare summer visitor, compared to Spain where it is easier to find. Occurs mainly in the Mértola and Elvas areas. It is also recorded occasionally as a passage migrant at various places, mainly coastal sites, usually in autumn. Kestrel, which may also breed colonially, can cause identification problems.

**Eleonora's Falcon.** A very scarce passage migrant, mainly in autumn. Most sightings are from the south-west coast. Breeding has been suspected but never proved.

**Purple Swamp-hen.** An extremely rare breeder, restricted to the Ria Formosa area (Ludo and Quinta do Lago), where a few pairs breed. It can be difficult to find, and there are restrictions to access in some areas. Exceptionally recorded outside the Algarve.

**Crested Coot.** A few records from the Algarve (Quinta do Lago) and western Alentejo (Santo André Lagoon) suggest that the species occurs more regularly than previously thought. Breeding status uncertain.

**Common Crane.** A winter visitor with a localised distribution in the Alentejo. Occurs regularly from November to February around Elvas, Castro Verde, Mourão and Barrancos, where it feeds both in open Holm Oak groves and cereal fields. It can be difficult to locate and should definitely not be disturbed.

**Little Bustard.** A fairly common resident breeder in southern Portugal, inhabiting mainly large open fields. Large flocks can be found in winter. May be decreasing, though it can still be found relatively easily around Castro Verde, Mourão, Elvas and the Tagus Estuary.

**Great Bustard.** Has decreased in recent years, due to habitat changes, but still occurs locally in small numbers throughout the Alentejo. Most regularly found on the Castro Verde plains, sometimes in flocks of 100 or more. Can be found displaying conspicuously in spring.

**Stone-curlew.** Dusk singing during the breeding season is often the first sign of its presence. At that time of year the species is widespread and occurs in both steppe areas and open oak woods. In winter, it tends to flock and is always difficult to detect and ascertain numbers. This resident species seems to be more common in the province of Alentejo.

**Collared Pratincole.** A local summer visitor to southern areas, breeding in open fields and fallowland, usually close to some water body. It breeds regularly at the Tagus Estuary, at Elvas, at Castro Marim and at Évora. Scarce on passage.

**Mediterranean Gull.** Regular and apparently increasing as a winter visitor. A few birds have been traced to Dutch breeding colonies. Some wintering sites are regularly occupied (e.g. the coastline west of Lisbon), but influxes occur, apparently due to weather conditions.

**Audouin's Gull.** Following a population increase in Spain, this species is now recorded regularly in early autumn, mainly in the Algarve.

**Caspian Tern.** A scarce but regular winter visitor in small numbers to wetlands on the south coast (Ria de Alvor, Faro and Castro Marim); up to twenty have been seen together at coastal roosts. Very scarce elsewhere, mainly as a passage migrant and, occasionally, in mid-summer. Nevertheless the Ria Formosa area may be one of the best places to find this species in Europe during the winter.

**Whiskered Tern.** An irregular breeder, its numbers and distribution are much dependent on winter rainfall and the resultant fluctuations in the water table in certain areas. The most likely place to see this species is at Boquilobo Marsh. It is also a scarce passage migrant and odd individuals have been seen in winter.

**Black-bellied Sandgrouse.** Nowadays a very rare resident species, probably due to changes in agricultural practices and hunting. Seen regularly between Castro Verde and Mértola, but sightings have decreased in recent years. Still occurs regularly at the International Tagus and Mourão, mainly in steppe-like habitat.

**Pin-tailed Sandgrouse.** Apparently once common, it is now an extremely rare species in Portugal, not seen every year. No 'guaranteed' sites can be indicated, although recent records come from the International Tagus area.

**Great Spotted Cuckoo.** A scarce summer visitor, which breeds locally. It is nowhere common, but seems to be slightly more frequent in the eastern part of the country. The best times to watch it (and hear it) are late February to early April (when adult birds are displaying) and June (when juveniles start to fly). Otherwise it is a shy bird which can be extremely difficult to locate. Scarce on passage.

**Scops Owl.** A summer visitor, mainly to the northernmost part of the country (Montesinho, International Douro, Gerês), where it is a common species, sometimes singing in the middle of town parks. Less common in southern Portugal as a breeding species, although it occurs regularly in the Algarve on autumn migration. Like most owls, more often heard than seen.

**Eagle Owl.** A rare resident, which occurs extremely locally throughout the country, but mainly in remote inland areas, like Barrancos, International Tagus and International Douro. Usually it is difficult to locate, due to its nocturnal habits; the distinctive song may be the first and only sign of its presence.

**Red-necked Nightjar.** A fairly common summer visitor, except to the north-western part of the country. Occurs in a variety of habitats, but most often in a mixed landscape of woods and dry open fields. Best located from late April to early July, at Tagus Estuary, International Tagus and in the Algarve.

**Pallid Swift.** A common summer visitor mainly to the southern half of the country, although it occurs as far north as Aveiro. It is much overlooked because of confusion with Swift. There are sizeable colonies in the cities of Lisbon, Setúbal, Elvas and Faro, and it occurs regularly at Sagres, at Arrábida and at the Tagus and Sado Estuaries.

**Alpine Swift.** A common summer visitor to the south-west coast and International Douro areas, which also breeds locally in other areas. Occurs regularly as a passage migrant over most of the country.

**White-rumped Swift.** As in Spain, there has been a recent increase in reports of this species, mainly from the southern half of the country. It is still very rare with only about a dozen records to date. Found breeding near Mértola in summer 1995.

**Roller.** An uncommon summer visitor to open areas in the eastern part of the country. It is relatively common around Elvas and at Castro Verde and occurs also at Mourão and Miranda do Douro. On autumn migration, it is regularly seen at Sagres and occasionally in other areas.

**Wryneck.** An uncommon summer visitor and breeding species, which is most easily detected in April and May by its song. Best looked for in the north-eastern part of Portugal, like International Douro and

Montesinho, where it occurs in open habitats with some trees. It is regularly observed as a passage migrant in autumn and individuals have been recorded in winter in the southern half of the country.

**Calandra Lark.** A resident bird, which breeds in open, steppe-like areas. Occurs mainly at Évora, Castro Verde, Mourão and the International Tagus, although it can be seen regularly in other areas with suitable habitat.

**Short-toed Lark.** A common summer visitor, breeding mainly in dry open habitats, most numerous in the southern half of the country, although it is possibly absent only from the north-western part of the country.

**Lesser Short-toed Lark.** A small population occurs in the Castro Marim area, where it breeds in dry saltmarsh and is present throughout the year. Extremely rare elsewhere.

**Thekla Lark.** A common resident, more widespread in the eastern half of the country. It seems to prefer rocky, uncultivated areas, sometimes with few trees. Best looked for near Castro Verde, Mértola and International Tagus, but it is quite common from Sagres north to Cape Sardão as well. In the Elvas area, both 'crested' species are common, allowing for comparison.

**Crag Martin.** A resident breeder in the eastern half of the country, which occurs mainly in river valleys. Look for them near large dams, rocky outcrops, stone bridges and old castles. In winter, it has a more widespread distribution and occurs in wetlands and coastal cliffs, where it may form large roosts.

**Red-rumped Swallow.** A summer visitor breeding in small numbers throughout the country. It is most numerous in the south, particularly at certain sites near the Spanish border, like Barrancos, International Tagus and Mértola. It nests under stone bridges, in old castles and ruins.

**Tawny Pipit.** A summer visitor with a localised distribution. It occurs mainly in the northern hills (e.g. Gerês and Montesinho), where it is fairly common. In the Alentejo plains it is a scarce bird, except near the coast, where it seems to be more numerous. Occurs as a passage migrant in coastal areas, especially in autumn.

**Alpine Accentor.** A very scarce winter visitor with an extremely localised distribution; regular sightings however occur at Cape Saint Vincent lighthouse, at the rocky bluffs on International Tagus (notably at Vila Velha de Ródão) and some of the castles of eastern Portugal (e.g. Marvão, near Portalegre).

**Rufous Bushchat.** A scarce summer visitor, which prefers river valleys with Sun Rose and Oleander. It is restricted to the south-eastern part of the country. A late breeder, arriving in May, it should be looked for in Castro Verde, Mértola and Mourão. Rather rare on passage.

**Bluethroat.** Common but localised passage migrant and winter visitor to coastal wetland areas, such as Tagus and Sado Estuaries and the Ria Formosa area.

**Black-eared Wheatear.** A summer visitor, which is most common in the Alentejo (Castro Verde, Mértola, Barrancos and Mourão) and rather scarce elsewhere. It occurs in a variety of habitats, mainly in open country.

**Black Wheatear.** A resident species, largely restricted to the International Tagus, where it is not uncommon in the rocky river valley. Portas de Ródão and International Tagus are good sites for this species, though it occurs very locally in other areas, like International Douro.

**Rock Thrush.** Breeds in the high mountains of the northern part of the country, but the breeding density is very low indeed. The best places to look for it are the Gerês National Park and the Montesinho area, but any sighting of this bird will require either good luck or a long walk over the 'tops'. Occasionally recorded on passage at coastal sites.

**Blue Rock Thrush.** A resident species, most commonly found in deep rocky river valleys, and along rocky coasts, but also to be found locally on inland castles. Can be most easily located on the steep slopes of places like Arrábida and Sagres, where it is seen at sea level, and in remote inland areas, like Barrancos, Miranda do Douro, and the International Tagus valley.

**Savi's Warbler.** A rather localised summer visitor to reedbed areas. It is common at Santo André and Mondego Marshes, but is rather scarce elsewhere (Ria de Aveiro, Tagus Estuary and Boquilobo Marsh). Rarely seen on migration.

**Olivaceous Warbler.** A rare summer visitor, largely confined to the south-easternmost areas. Due to its rarity and to the lack of information available, it is not possible to indicate specific sites. However, there have been some records from the region between the river Guadiana and the Spanish border, east of Beja, around Sobral da Adiça and Vila Verde de Ficalho, and also around Castro Marim.

**Spectacled Warbler.** An uncommon breeding species with a localised distribution. Although it is a summer migrant, it arrives very early, usually in late February or early March. Best looked for in Castro Marim (where it breeds in saltmarsh areas) or east of Mértola (where it occurs in low scrub). It is also known from Freixo de Espada à Cinta, in the International Douro and from Cape Saint Vincent.

**Subalpine Warbler.** A common summer visitor to the north-eastern province of Trás-os-Montes, where, remarkably, it may be the most numerous warbler in bushy areas (e.g. Miranda do Douro and Montesinho). Much less common in the eastern Alentejo, though it can be found, mainly in Sun Rose scrub, near Mértola or Mourão. Not uncommon on passage, often seen as early as mid-March in breeding areas.

**Orphean Warbler.** Uncommon as a breeding species over most of the country. Its distribution is patchy and it is unlikely to be seen in most areas. It can, however, be found regularly in Miranda do Douro and in the International Tagus valley, mainly in open woods, and in valleys north of Tavira and Castro Marim, as far north as Mértola.

**Bonelli's Warbler.** A summer visitor which occurs mainly in the northern part of the country (Gerês, Miranda do Douro and Montesinho), where it is rather numerous in Pyrenean Oak and

Maritime/Scots Pine woods although it can occur in other habitats as well. In the south it is scarce and is most often seen in Cork Oak or Maritime Pine woods, with understorey, as the Sado Estuary. Occurs regularly on autumn migration.

**Penduline Tit.** A winter visitor to reedbed areas, occurring locally over most of southern Portugal. If looked for in suitable habitat, can be found in Tagus and Sado Estuaries, at Santo André Lagoon and, occasionally, at Boquilobo Marsh. Breeds very locally near Elvas.

**Red-backed Shrike.** A late summer visitor (arriving mid May) to the northernmost part of the country. In Gerês it is common and occurs in open plateaus throughout the park, whereas in Montesinho it is rather uncommon and its habitat is not yet very well defined. Not usually recorded outside its breeding area.

**Red-billed Chough.** A resident species which in Portugal is restricted to four sites: Sagres, where it breeds in coastal rocks; Serras de Aire e Candeeiros (near Leiria, in the central part of the country), where it breeds in vertical caves; Gerês National Park, where it occurs in rocky areas; and in the north-east, where it occurs in the rocky valleys of the river Douro and tributaries. In the latter site, it is quite common, while in the other sites it is rather scarce.

**Spanish Sparrow.** Breeds colonially in the eastern half of Portugal and may be expanding its range. Occurs in a variety of habitats, such as telegraph poles, stork nests and small woods. Most easily found at International Tagus, Mourão and Mértola. Very localised in winter, sometimes being seen near the coast.

**Rock Sparrow.** A widespread resident with a localised distribution. Occurs in a variety of habitats, from rocky valleys to Cork Oak woods. May be seen at times in Sand Martin colonies. Rather frequent in the woods around the Tagus and Sado Estuaries, but present in most of the sites described in this book.

**Common Waxbill.** This African species was introduced in the late 1960s and is now widespread over most of the country. It is particularly common in wetland areas, including estuaries, riversides, reedbeds and lagoons with dense cover along the shores.

**Red Avadavat.** Another introduced bird (from Asia), which is common in the Elvas area, along riverine vegetation or in reeds. It also occurs in the Tagus Estuary.

**Rock Bunting.** A resident species which is very common in the northern provinces, especially in wild hilly country, and relatively uncommon and localised in the southern half of Portugal, where it is restricted to some small rocky valleys. The best sites to look for it are undoubtedly Gerês and Montesinho.

**Ortolan Bunting.** A summer visitor to the higher mountains in the northern part of the country. It breeds in Gerês, Montesinho and Serra da Estrela. In the southern part of Portugal, it occurs mainly on migration, regularly in autumn and, less frequently, in spring.

# Selective Species List for Madeira

**Fea's / Zino's Petrel.** These two closely related *Pterodroma* petrels breed in the archipelago but differ in breeding habitat and phenology. Zino's Petrel is now so rare that the regular sightings of *Pterodroma* petrels off the south coast of mainland Madeira and at sea between Funchal and Porto Santo are assumed to be Fea's Petrel, which breeds on Bugio, the southernmost of the Desertas islands. It has been seen off Ponta da Cruz and more regularly from the Porto Santo ferry.

**Bulwer's Petrel.** Breeds in moderate numbers on islets off eastern Madeira and in much larger numbers on the Desertas, Porto Santo and especially Selvagem Grande. Summer and autumn observations are regular off Funchal and Ponta da Cruz, just west of Funchal. Often seen from boats.

**Cory's Shearwater.** Breeds on mainland Madeira as well as on the Desertas and on Porto Santo. The largest population in the archipelago is on Selvagem Grande where about 10,000 pairs breed annually. The species can be seen all year round from many of the mainland's headlands and is often heard calling at night.

**Little Shearwater.** Breeds in small numbers on islets off eastern Madeira, the Desertas and Porto Santo, although accurate counts are not available. On Selvagem Grande about 1000 pairs breed annually. Small numbers are seen from Ponta da Cruz, just west of Funchal and larger numbers are often found when sailing to Porto Santo and back, especially towards dusk. The best period seems to be June to September, when young leave the nest for nearby waters.

**White-faced Storm Petrel.** The Selvagem Islands hold the only breeding birds in the Madeiran archipelago with about 10,000 pairs. Present from January, probably dispersing in late summer. Very few have ever been seen either from land or from boats except close to their breeding sites but Ponta da Cruz, just west of Funchal, is certainly worth trying in onshore winds.

**Madeiran Storm Petrel.** Breeds in small numbers on islets off eastern Madeira and in possibly larger numbers on Porto Santo and the Desertas. About 500 pairs breed on Selvagem Grande. Probably at least two populations are involved, the research indicating that breeding sites appear to be occupied almost continuously. Land-based seawatches indicate that it is very scarce inshore but at Ponta da Cruz, a few km west of Funchal, the species has been recorded in autumn. It is important to remember that Storm Petrels are seen in these waters and that many white-rumped petrel sightings are likely to be of the latter species. Sometimes it is seen from boats plying between Funchal and Porto Santo, especially between June and September.

**Roseate Tern.** A summer visitor in very small numbers to the Madeiran archipelago. Breeding may occur. Worth watching for in Funchal harbour, at Caniçal and at the eastern tip of Madeira. It also occurs around the Deserta islands and Selvagem pequena.

**Long-toed Pigeon.** About 1000 of these unique birds exist on Madeira island, their habitat in the main being the extensive laurel forest. The best places to observe the species are steep-sided forest-clad valleys.

Typical sites include Fajã da Nogueira and Balcões / Ribeiro Frio on the ER103. It also occurs in north-western Madeira around Vale da Ribeira da Janela, especially at Rabaçal on the ER204.

**Plain Swift.** A Macaronesian species, breeding in rocky clefts of the many 'ribeiras', along the road-cuttings east of Funchal and at least one seacliff site near Câmara de Lobos, west of Funchal. Also breeds or roosts on small rocky islets close inshore near Funchal. Largely absent in winter. It appears not to occur on the Desertas or Selvagem islands.

**Berthelot's Pipit.** This is an endemic Macaronesian species possibly most closely related to Tawny Pipit. It frequents dry rocky habitat in eastern Madeira, on the Deserta islands and on the Selvagem islands as well. There are at least two subspecies, namely *berthelotii* on the Selvagem islands and *madeirensis* on Madeira and the Desertas. The most reliable sites to find it are at Caniçal and Ponta de São Lourenço, both at the eastern tip of mainland Madeira.

**Spectacled Warbler.** Limited to the eastern end of Madeira and the island of Porto Santo, this species (subspecies *bella*) is resident in very small numbers. Look for it east of Caniçal.

**Firecrest.** This is a subspecies (*madeirensis*) which can easily be distinguished in the field. It is largely found in Laurel forest, a habitat it shares with Long-toed Pigeon and Madeiran Chaffinch. Reliable sites include Fajã da Nogueira and Balcões / Ribeiro Frio on the ER103. It also occurs along the ER204 around Rabaçal and in other Laurel forest sites. Listen out for its call.

**Spanish Sparrow.** This species, which was introduced about 70 years ago, occupies a wide variety of habitat and can be seen in many villages and cultivated areas, especially on Porto Santo and the eastern end of Madeira.

**Rock Sparrow.** In the Madeiran archipelago it is limited to Madeira and Porto Santo. This subspecies (*madeirensis*), which is basically not distinguishable from the nominate race, is associated with the dry stony habitats beloved of Berthelot's Pipit. The most reliable site to locate it is at the extreme eastern tip of Madeira, just west of Ponta de São Lourenço.

**Chaffinch.** This is a subspecies of Chaffinch (*madeirensis*), which together with the Azorean Chaffinch most closely resemble North African races. It is limited to mainland Madeira, being found in both Pine and Laurel forest. Reliable sites to locate it include Ribeiro Frio and Fajã da Nogueira on the ER103 and around Poiso cross-roads. It also occurs on the route to Curral das Freiras. Listen out for its distinctive 'dialect'.

**Canary.** Limited to Macaronesian islands in its wild state, this close relative to Serin (which does not occur on Madeira) frequents a wide variety of habitat and occurs over a wide range of altitude. Close to Funchal it can be seen at Ponta da Cruz.

# Status of Sought-after Species at the Eighteen Major Sites in Mainland Portugal

The following table gives the migratory, breeding and abundance status of 168 species found at some or all of the major sites described. However, certain other species, listed below, are so generally widespread and common over most of Portugal that they have been omitted from the table. Obviously, all species occurring as vagrants have also been excluded, but are included in the full species list.

The following abbreviations are used in the table (uppercase letters mean that the species is fairly common in the area and is likely to be found in suitable habitat; lowercase letters mean the species is scarce at a particular site and that it may be difficult to find):

R/r  = common resident / scarce resident
S/s  = common summer visitor / scarce summer visitor
P/p  = common on passage / scarce on passage
W/w  = common winter visitor / scarce winter visitor
A  = does not occur regularly but records are known from the area

Any combination of these categories may be used, e.g.:

Sw  = common in summer and scarce in winter, etc.

| | 1 | 2 | 3 | 4 | 5 | 6 | 7 | 8 | 9 | 10 | 11 | 12 | 13 | 14 | 15 | 16 | 17 | 18 |
|---|---|---|---|---|---|---|---|---|---|---|---|---|---|---|---|---|---|---|
| Black-necked Grebe | | | | w | | A | w | | | W | w | A | | | | w | w | |
| Shag | | | | w | | | | r | r | | | | | | | | | r |
| Little Bittern | | | | s | | S | s | | s | s | S | s | | | | p | S | |
| Black-crowned Night Heron | | | | | | S | A | r | A | p | A | s | | | A | p | p | p |
| Purple Heron | | | | S | | S | S | | s | S | S | | | s | s | p | s | p |
| Black Stork | A | s | s | | S | A | A | A | A | A | A | s | s | | r | p | p | |
| Spoonbill | | | | wp | | S | p | A | | p | P | | | | | S | r | |
| Greater Flamingo | | | | wp | | | R | A | | R | P | | | | | R | R | |
| Gadwall | w | | | Ws | | w | w | | w | W | w | w | r | | r | w | W | |
| Garganey | | | | wp | | s | p | | p | wp | | | | | | p | p | |
| Red-crested Pochard | | | | w | | r | r | | | p | Ws | w | | | r | p | w | p |
| Honey Buzzard | s | s | s | | | A | p | | A | p | | | | | | A | | P |
| Black-shouldered Kite | | A | | | r | P | r | A | P | | r | r | r | r | r | | w | P |
| Red Kite | A | r | S | wp | Ws | A | p | | | A | A | w | Ws | Ws | w | A | p | p |
| Egyptian Vulture | A | s | S | | S | | | | P | | A | | p | | s | p | | p |
| Griffon Vulture | A | A | R | | R | | A | A | | | | | r | R | r | A | p | p |
| Black Vulture | | A | A | | r | | | | | A | | A | A | r | r | | | A |
| Short-toed Eagle | s | s | s | P | s | s | s | P | P | s | p | s | s | s | s | p | sp | P |
| Marsh Harrier | | | | R | | p | Ws | A | p | r | r | w | | | p | r | W | p |
| Goshawk | r | | r | r | | A | w | w | w | | A | | | | A | r | | p |
| Golden Eagle | r | r | r | | r | | | | | | | | r | r | r | | p | p |
| Booted Eagle | s | A | s | s | s | s | s | P | P | r | p | s | s | | s | p | p | p |

1 - Peneda-Gerês; 2 - Montesinho; 3 - Internacional Douro; 4 - Ria de Aveiro; 5 - Internacional Tagus; 6 - Boquilobo Marsh; 7 - Tagus Estuary; 8 - Lisbon and Estoril Coast; 9 - Cape Espichel and Arrábida; 10 - Sado Estuary; 11 - Santo André Lagoon; 12 - Elvas Plains; 13 - Mourão; 14 - Barrancos; 15 - Castro Verde and Mértola; 16 - Castro Marim; 17 - Ria Formosa; 18 - Sagres and Cape St Vincent

| | 1 | 2 | 3 | 4 | 5 | 6 | 7 | 8 | 9 | 10 | 11 | 12 | 13 | 14 | 15 | 16 | 17 | 18 |
|---|---|---|---|---|---|---|---|---|---|---|---|---|---|---|---|---|---|---|
| Melodious Warbler | s | S | S | S | s | S | SP | | SP | SP | SP | S | | | s | rp | SP | P |
| Spectacled Warbler | | | s | | | | | | A | | | | | | s | s | P | P |
| Subalpine Warbler | s | S | S | | s | A | P | A | P | P | P | | s | | s | P | P | P |
| Orphean Warbler | | s | s | | s | | | | A | | | | | s | s | P | P | |
| Bonelli's Warbler | S | S | S | P | | | P | | P | sp | P | | | s | | P | P | P |
| Firecrest | r | R | | W | | w | w | r | w | w | w | | | w | w | w | W | |
| Crested Tit | R | R | R | R | | | r | | r | R | r | r | r | r | r | r | r | r |
| Penduline Tit | | | | w | | w | W | | w | w | w | s | | | | | W | |
| Golden Oriole | S | S | S | s | S | S | s | A | s | s | s | s | s | s | S | P | sp | P |
| Red-backed Shrike | S | s | | | | | | | | | A | | | | | | | A |
| Chough | r | | R | | | | A | | A | | | | | | | | | r |
| Raven | r | R | R | | R | | A | | r | | | r | r | r | R | A | | r |
| Spanish Sparrow | | A | s | | Sw | | A | | P | w | | s | s | s | R | | | P |
| Rock Sparrow | r | r | r | | R | r | R | | r | r | r | r | r | R | r | r | | |
| Common Waxbill | | | | R | | R | R | r | r | R | R | r | | | r | r | R | r |
| Crossbill | r | r | | P | | | P | P | P | | A | | | | | r | P | P |
| Hawfinch | A | r | R | A | r | r | r | A | r | r | A | | | r | | r | r | |
| Cirl Bunting | r | R | R | r | r | | r | | R | R | r | r | s | r | r | r | r | |
| Rock Bunting | R | R | R | | r | | | | r | | | r | r | r | r | r | | |
| Ortolan Bunting | S | S | | | | P | P | P | P | A | P | | | | | P | P | P |

1 - Peneda-Gerês; 2 - Montesinho; 3 - Internacional Douro; 4 - Ria de Aveiro; 5 - Internacional Tagus; 6 - Boquilobo Marsh; 7 - Tagus Estuary; 8 - Lisbon and Estoril Coast; 9 - Cape Espichel and Arrábida; 10 - Sado Estuary; 11 - Santo André Lagoon; 12 - Elvas Plains; 13 - Mourão; 14 - Barrancos; 15 - Castro Verde and Mértola; 16 - Castro Marim; 17 - Ria Formosa; 18 - Sagres and Cape St Vincent

| | 1 | 2 | 3 | 4 | 5 | 6 | 7 | 8 | 9 | 10 | 11 | 12 | 13 | 14 | 15 | 16 | 17 | 18 |
|---|---|---|---|---|---|---|---|---|---|---|---|---|---|---|---|---|---|---|
| Pomarine Skua | | | | | | | | wp | p | p | p | | | | | | | p |
| Great Skua | | | | w | | | | w | w | | | | | | | | w | p |
| Mediterranean Gull | | | | w | | | P | WP | p | wp | wp | | | | | p | WP | p |
| Little Gull | | | | P | | | P | wp | p | p | A | | | | | p | wp | |
| Audouin's Gull | | | | | | | | p | | | | | | | | p | p | p |
| Yellow-legged Gull | | | | Ws | | w | p | R | R | R | R | | | | | WP | R | R |
| Gull-billed Tern | | | | P | | A | p | sP | | p | p | | | | | p | p | |
| Caspian Tern | | | | | | | p | | | | A | | | | | pw | wp | p |
| Whiskered Tern | | | | | | S | | | | | | | | | | p | p | |
| Black Tern | | | P | P | P | | P | P | P | p | p | | | | | p | p | p |
| Black-bellied Sandgrouse | | | | | | | | | | | | | r | | r | | | |
| Pin-tailed Sandgrouse | | | | | | | | | | | | | A | | | | | |
| Great Spotted Cuckoo | s | | s | s | s | s | s | p | p | s | s | s | s | s | s | p | p | p |
| Scops Owl | S | S | S | s | s | | | | p | s | A | s | s | s | s | p | | s |
| Eagle Owl | r | r | R | r | r | | | | | | | | r | r | r | | | p |
| Short-eared Owl | | A | | w | | wp | w | A | A | w | w | | | | A | | w | p |
| European Nightjar | s | S | s | s | | s | s | | | s | sp | | | | | p | | |
| Red-necked Nightjar | | s | s | | | s | S | | | s | sp | s | s | s | s | s | S | S |
| Pallid Swift | | | | S | | | S | S | S | S | A | s | s | s | s | SP | s | S |
| Alpine Swift | | | S | p | s | sp | p | p | s | p | A | | | | r | p | p | S |
| White-rumped Swift | | | | | | | A | | | | | | A | A | | | | |
| Roller | p | A | s | | | | p | p | p | p | p | S | S | s | S | p | p | p |

1 - Peneda-Gerês; 2 - Montesinho; 3 - Internacional Douro; 4 - Ria de Aveiro; 5 - Internacional Tagus; 6 - Boquilobo Marsh; 7 - Tagus Estuary; 8 - Lisbon and Estoril Coast; 9 - Cape Espichel and Arrábida; 10 - Sado Estuary; 11 - Santo André Lagoon; 12 - Elvas Plains; 13 - Mourão; 14 - Barrancos; 15 - Castro Verde and Mértola; 16 - Castro Marim; 17 - Ria Formosa; 18 - Sagres and Cape St Vincent

| | 1 | 2 | 3 | 4 | 5 | 6 | 7 | 8 | 9 | 10 | 11 | 12 | 13 | 14 | 15 | 16 | 17 | 18 |
|---|---|---|---|---|---|---|---|---|---|---|---|---|---|---|---|---|---|---|
| Lesser Spotted Woodpecker | | | | | | R | r | | | | | | | | | | | |
| Wryneck | s | S | S | P | | A | r | | P | | P | | | r | r | P | P | P |
| Calandra Lark | | r | r | | R | | r | | | | | r | R | r | R | r | | |
| Short-toed Lark | | s | s | s | S | | S | A | P | s | s | s | S | | S | SP | SP | P |
| Lesser Short-toed Lark | | | | | | | | | | | | | | | | r | | |
| Crested Lark | r | r | | r | | R | R | r | r | R | R | R | r | | r | R | R | |
| Thekla Lark | | r | R | | R | | | | | r | r | R | R | R | R | r | r | R |
| Crag Martin | r | S | R | w | R | w | | w | w | w | | r | r | R | R | P | w | w |
| Red-rumped Swallow | s | s | s | P | S | s | s | | s | s | P | s | S | S | S | sp | sp | P |
| Tawny Pipit | S | S | | P | | | sp | | P | P | P | | | | s | sp | P | P |
| Water Pipit | w | Ws | | W | | w | W | | w | W | W | | | | | Wp | W | |
| Dipper | r | r | | | | | | | | | | | | | | | | |
| Alpine Accentor | w | | | | | | | w | w | | | | | | | | | w |
| Rufous Bushchat | | | | | | | | | | | | s | s | | s | | sp | P |
| Bluethroat | | | | wp | | p | WP | | p | WP | Pw | | | | | Wp | WP | P |
| Black-eared Wheatear | s | s | S | P | s | P | A | | | s | | S | S | S | S | P | sP | P |
| Black Wheatear | | r | r | | r | | | | | | | | | r | | | | |
| Rock Thrush | s | | | | | | | | p | | | | | | | | | p |
| Blue Rock Thrush | r | r | r | | r | | r | r | r | | | r | r | r | r | r | | R |
| Savi's Warbler | | | | | | s | s | | | s | S | | | | r | p | A | |
| Great Reed Warbler | | | | S | | S | S | | s | S | S | S | | | s | rp | sP | |
| Olivaceous Warbler | | | | | | | A | | | A | A | | | | | p | | |

1 - Peneda-Gerês; 2 - Montesinho; 3 - Internacional Douro; 4 - Ria de Aveiro; 5 - Internacional Tagus; 6 - Boquilobo Marsh; 7 - Tagus Estuary; 8 - Lisbon and Estoril Coast; 9 - Cape Espichel and Arrábida; 10 - Sado Estuary; 11 - Santo André Lagoon; 12 - Elvas Plains; 13 - Mourão; 14 - Barrancos; 15 - Castro Verde and Mértola; 16 - Castro Marim; 17 - Ria Formosa; 18 - Sagres and Cape St Vincent

| | 1 | 2 | 3 | 4 | 5 | 6 | 7 | 8 | 9 | 10 | 11 | 12 | 13 | 14 | 15 | 16 | 17 | 18 |
|---|---|---|---|---|---|---|---|---|---|---|---|---|---|---|---|---|---|---|
| Bonelli's Eagle | A | A | r | | r | A | p | r | r | w | | | A | r | r | | wp | r |
| Osprey | | | p | w | p | wp | wp | p | p | wp | p | w | | | p | p | wp | p |
| Lesser Kestrel | | | | | s | | p | | p | A | | s | s | | s | p | | sp |
| Hobby | s | s | s | sP | | p | s | A | p | s | s | | | | s | p | p | p |
| Peregrine Falcon | r | r | r | w | r | w | wp | r | r | w | p | w | w | w | w | w | wp | r |
| Eleonora's Falcon | | | | | | | A | p | p | A | A | | | | | | | p |
| Quail | S | S | S | s | s | s | S | | | s | w | s | S | | S | Pw | | p |
| Crested Coot | | | | | | | | | | | w | | | | | | A | A |
| Purple Swamp-hen | | | | | | A | | | | A | A | | | | | | r | |
| Crane | | | | | | A | | | | | | w | W | W | W | | wp | |
| Little Bustard | A | A | r | | r | A | Ws | | | | P | R | R | | R | r | w | r |
| Great Bustard | A | | | | r | | P | | | | A | r | r | | R | A | A | A |
| Black-winged Stilt | | | | S | | S | S | | p | Sw | SP | S | s | | s | Sr | R | p |
| Avocet | | A | W | W | | A | W | w | | W | P | | | | | Rp | Ws | |
| Stone-curlew | | | r | r | r | | r | | | | r | r | r | | r | r | R | w |
| Collared Pratincole | | | | | | | S | | p | P | A | S | s | | s | s | S | |
| Little Ringed Plover | | | | sp | s | sp | sp | | p | sp | p | S | s | s | s | Ps | p | |
| Kentish Plover | | | | R | | | R | A | p | R | Sw | w | | | | R | R | p |
| Spotted Redshank | | | | p | | | Pw | | p | wp | p | | | | | Pw | wP | |
| Green Sandpiper | A | p | p | w | | w | w | p | w | w | p | | | W | w | pw | wp | |
| Wood Sandpiper | | | | p | | | p | p | p | p | p | | | | | p | p | |
| Arctic Skua | | | | p | | A | A | wP | wp | | | | | | | | w | p |

1 - Peneda-Gerês; 2 - Montesinho; 3 - Internacional Douro; 4 - Ria de Aveiro; 5 - International Tagus; 6 - Boquilobo Marsh; 7 - Tagus Estuary; 8 - Lisbon and Estoril Coast; 9 - Cape Espichel and Arrábida; 10 - Sado Estuary; 11 - Santo André Lagoon; 12 - Elvas Plains; 13 - Mourão; 14 - Barrancos; 15 - Castro Verde and Mértola; 16 - Castro Marim; 17 - Ria Formosa; 18 - Sagres and Cape St Vincent

# Mainland Portugal Full Species List

The list contains all known records of birds from mainland Portugal. Some records are undocumented, some mentioned merely as a name in passing and others from the last century, known only from anecdotal evidence. Thus the list does not attempt to be the definitive list for mainland Portugal.

Between 1987 and 1994, all rarities were verified by the Iberian Rarities Committee (IRC) and since January 1995 a Portuguese Rarities Committee (PRC) has been in operation. Records prior to 1987 which are undocumented or doubtful are currently under review. Records of rarities accepted by the IRC and more recently the PRC are marked with an asterisk. All other rarities are currently under review by the PRC.

r  – resident and regular breeder
s  – migrant breeder, present only in breeding period
p  – passage migrant
w  – regular winter visitor
A  – accidental species

1  – abundant
2  – common
3  – fairly common or widespread
4  – scarce or localised
5  – rare or very localised

| SPECIES | STATUS | ADDITIONAL INFORMATION |
|---|---|---|
| Red-throated Diver *Gavia stellata* | w5 p5 | usually only seen on seawatches |
| Black-throated Diver *Gavia arctica* | A | |
| Great Northern Diver *Gavia immer* | w5 p5 | * |
| Little Grebe *Tachybaptus ruficollis* | r3 | |
| Great Crested Grebe *Podiceps cristatus* | r4 p4 w4 | |
| Slavonian Grebe *Podiceps auritus* | A | |
| Black-necked Grebe *Podiceps nigricollis* | w4 | winters mainly in Sado Estuary |
| Black-browed Albatross *Diomedea melanophris* | A | |
| Wandering Albatross *Diomedea exulans* | A | |
| Fulmar *Fulmarus glacialis* | A | regularly found dead |
| Feas/Zino's Petrel *Pterodroma feae/madeira* | A | * |
| Bulwer's Petrel *Bulweria bulwerii* | A | *regular well offshore |
| Cory's Shearwater *Calonectris diomedea* | s2 p2 | occasionally seen in winter |
| Great Shearwater *Puffinus gravis* | p5 | regular well offshore |
| Sooty Shearwater *Puffinus griseus* | p4 | |
| Manx Shearwater *Puffinus puffinus* | w4 p4 | |
| Balearic Shearwater *Puffinus mauretanicus* | w2 p2 | sometimes seen in summer |
| Little Shearwater *Puffinus assimilis* | A | *regular well offshore |
| Wilson's Storm Petrel *Oceanites oceanicus* | A | *regular within 20km in late summer |
| White-faced Storm Petrel *Pelagodroma marina* | A | * |
| Storm Petrel *Hydrobates pelagicus* | w4 p4 | |
| Leach's Storm Petrel *Oceanodroma leucorhoa* | w5 | *usually found dead after storms |
| Madeiran Storm Petrel *Oceanodroma castro* | r5 | apparently limited to 1 breeding site |

| SPECIES | STATUS | ADDITIONAL INFORMATION |
|---|---|---|
| Red-billed Tropicbird *Phaethon aethereus* | A | * |
| Brown Booby *Sula leucogaster* | A | * |
| Gannet *Morus bassanus* | w1 p1 | often seen in summer |
| Cormorant *Phalacrocorax carbo* | w1 p1 | |
| Shag *Phalacrocorax aristotelis* | r3 | |
| White Pelican *Pelecanus onocrotalus* | A | *probably an escaped bird |
| Bittern *Botaurus stellaris* | w5 | has bred |
| Little Bittern *Ixobrychus minutus* | s3 | |
| Black-crowned Night Heron | | |
|    *Nycticorax nycticorax* | s5 p5 | breeds only at two locations |
| Squacco Heron *Ardeola ralloides* | s5 p5 | occasionally seen in winter |
| Cattle Egret *Bubulcus ibis* | r1 | |
| Western Reef Egret *Egretta gularis* | A | * |
| Little Egret *Egretta garzetta* | r2 | |
| Great White Egret *Egretta alba* | w5 | * apparently increasing |
| Grey Heron *Ardea cinerea* | r3 w2 | |
| Purple Heron *Ardea purpurea* | s3 | |
| Black Stork *Ciconia nigra* | s4 w5 | |
| White Stork *Ciconia ciconia* | s1 p1 w3 | |
| Glossy Ibis *Plegadis falcinellus* | p5 | apparently increasing |
| Spoonbill *Platalea leucorodia* | s5 p4 w4 | breeds only at four sites; few pairs |
| Greater Flamingo *Phoenicopterus ruber* | r4 p4 | does not breed, locally common |
| Mute Swan *Cygnus olor* | A | |
| Bewick's Swan *Cygnus columbianus* | A | |
| Whooper Swan *Cygnus cygnus* | A | * |
| Bean Goose *Anser fabalis* | A | |
| White-fronted Goose *Anser albifrons* | A | * |
| Greylag Goose *Anser anser* | w4 | winters mainly in Tagus Estuary |
| Barnacle Goose *Branta leucopsis* | A | * |
| Brent Goose *Branta bernicla* | w5 | scarce and irregular |
| Ruddy Shelduck *Tadorna ferruginea* | A | * |
| Shelduck *Tadorna tadorna* | w5 | |
| Wigeon *Anas penelope* | w2 | |
| American Wigeon *Anas americana* | A | |
| Falcated Duck *Anas falcata* | A | * |
| Gadwall *Anas strepera* | r4 w3 | |
| Teal *Anas crecca* | w1 | American race also recorded |
| Mallard *Anas platyrhynchos* | r2 w1 | |
| Pintail *Anas acuta* | w3 | |
| Garganey *Anas querquedula* | s5 p4 w5 | |
| Blue-winged Teal *Anas discors* | A | * |
| Shoveler *Anas clypeata* | r5 w1 | |
| Marbled Duck *Marmaronetta angustirostris* | A | * |
| Red-crested Pochard *Netta rufina* | r5 w4 | winter numbers variable |
| Pochard *Aythya ferina* | r5 w3 | |
| Ring-necked Duck *Aythya collaris* | A | |
| Ferruginous Duck *Aythya nyroca* | w5 | |
| Tufted Duck *Aythya fuligula* | w3 | |
| Scaup *Aythya marila* | w5 | |

| SPECIES | STATUS | ADDITIONAL INFORMATION |
|---|---|---|
| Ring-necked Duck *Aythya affinis* | A | * |
| Common Eider *Somateria mollissima* | A | * |
| Long-tailed Duck *Clangula hyemalis* | A | * |
| Black Scoter *Melanitta nigra* | w3 | |
| Velvet Scoter *Melanitta fusca* | A | |
| Bufflehead *Bucephala albeola* | A | * |
| Goldeneye *Bucephala clangula* | A | |
| Smew *Mergus albellus* | A | |
| Red-breasted Merganser *Mergus serrator* | w4 | common in Sado Estuary only |
| Goosander *Mergus merganser* | A | |
| Ruddy Duck *Oxyura jamaicensis* | A | * |
| White-headed Duck *Oxyura leucocephala* | A | * |
| Honey-buzzard *Pernis apivorus* | s4 p3 | common at Sagres in autumn |
| Black-shouldered Kite *Elanus caeruleus* | r3 | |
| Black Kite *Milvus migrans* | s2 p2 | |
| Red Kite *Milvus milvus* | r4 w3 | |
| White-tailed Eagle *Haliaeetus albicilla* | A | |
| Lammergeier *Gypaetus barbatus* | A | last record 19th century |
| Egyptian Vulture *Neophron percnopterus* | s4 p4 | |
| Griffon Vulture *Gyps fulvus* | r4 p4 | locally common |
| Ruppell's Vulture *Gyps rueppellii* | A | * |
| Black Vulture *Aegypius monachus* | r5 | no recent breeding records |
| Short-toed Eagle *Circaetus gallicus* | s3 p3 | |
| Marsh Harrier *Circus aeruginosus* | r3 w3 | |
| Hen Harrier *Circus cyaneus* | r5 w3 | |
| Montagu's Harrier *Circus pygargus* | s2 p3 | |
| Goshawk *Accipiter gentilis* | r4 | occurs mainly in the North |
| Sparrowhawk *Accipiter nisus* | r3 p3 | occurs mainly in the North |
| Buzzard *Buteo buteo* | r2 p3 | |
| Long-legged Buzzard *Buteo rufinus* | A | |
| Lesser Spotted Eagle *Aquila pomarina* | A | |
| Greater Spotted Eagle *Aquila clanga* | A | |
| Spanish Imperial Eagle *Aquila adalberti* | r5 | on verge of extinction |
| Golden Eagle *Aquila chrysaetos* | r4 | more widespread in northeast |
| Booted Eagle *Hieraaetus pennatus* | s3 p2 w5 | |
| Bonelli's Eagle *Hieraaetus fasciatus* | r4 | more widespread in northeast |
| Osprey *Pandion haliaetus* | r5 p3 w4 | |
| Lesser Kestrel *Falco naumanni* | s5 p5 | dramatic decrease, now very local |
| Kestrel *Falco tinnunculus* | r2 | |
| Red-footed Falcon *Falco vespertinus* | A | |
| Merlin *Falco columbarius* | w4 | |
| Hobby *Falco subbuteo* | s3 p3 | |
| Eleonora's Falcon *Falco eleonorae* | p5 | |
| Lanner Falcon *Falco biarmicus* | A | |
| Gyr Falcon *Falco rusticolus* | A | * |
| Peregrine Falcon *Falco peregrinus* | r4 w4 | |
| Red-legged Partridge *Alectoris rufa* | r3 | |
| Grey Partridge *Perdix perdix* | ? | probably extinct |
| Quail *Coturnix coturnix* | s3 w5 | winters locally |

| SPECIES | STATUS | ADDITIONAL INFORMATION |
|---|---|---|
| Small Button-quail *Turnix sylvatica* | ? | status uncertain |
| Water Rail *Rallus aquaticus* | r3 | |
| Spotted Crake *Porzana porzana* | p5 w5 | |
| Little Crake *Porzana parva* | A | |
| Baillon's Crake *Porzana pusilla* | s5 | |
| Corncrake *Crex crex* | A | one recent documented record |
| Moorhen *Gallinula chloropus* | r2 | |
| Allen's Gallinule *Porphyrula alleni* | A | * |
| Purple Swamp-hen *Porphyrio porphyrio* | r5 | only breeds in the Algarve |
| Coot *Fulica atra* | r3 w2 | |
| American Coot *Fulica americana* | A | * |
| Crested Coot *Fulica cristata* | A | * |
| Common Crane *Grus grus* | w4 | |
| Demoiselle Crane *Anthropoides virgo* | A | last recorded 19th century |
| Little Bustard *Tetrax tetrax* | r3 w3 | |
| Great Bustard *Otis tarda* | r4 | |
| Oystercatcher *Haematopus ostralegus* | w4 | |
| Black-winged Stilt *Himantopus himantopus* | s2 p2 w4 | locally overwinters in the south |
| Avocet *Recurvirostra avosetta* | r5 w2 | breeds mainly at Castro Marim |
| Stone-curlew *Burhinus oedicnemus* | r4 w4 | |
| Cream-coloured Courser *Cursorius cursor* | A | * |
| Collared Pratincole *Glareola pratincola* | s4 | |
| Little Ringed Plover *Charadrius dubius* | p3 s3 w5 | |
| Ringed Plover *Charadrius hiaticula* | w1 p1 | |
| Kentish Plover *Charadrius alexandrinus* | r2 p2 | |
| Dotterel *Charadrius morinellus* | p5 | |
| American Golden Plover *Pluvialis dominica* | A | * |
| Golden Plover *Pluvialis apricaria* | w3 | |
| Grey Plover *Pluvialis squatarola* | w1 p1 | |
| Sociable Plover *Vanellus gregarius* | A | * |
| Lapwing *Vanellus vanellus* | r5 w2 | breeds occasionally in the south |
| Knot *Calidris canutus* | w4 p2 | |
| Sanderling *Calidris alba* | w3 p2 | |
| Semi-palmated Sandpiper *Calidris pusilla* | A | * |
| Little Stint *Calidris minuta* | w4 p3 | |
| Temminck's Stint *Calidris temminckii* | p5 | |
| Pectoral Sandpiper *Calidris melanotos* | A | * |
| Curlew Sandpiper *Calidris ferruginea* | p3 | |
| Purple Sandpiper *Calidris maritima* | w5 | |
| Dunlin *Calidris alpina* | w1 p1 | |
| Broad-billed Sandpiper *Limicola falcinellus* | A | |
| Buff-breasted Sandpiper *Tryngites subruficollis* | A | * |
| Ruff *Philomachus pugnax* | w5 p3 | |
| Jack Snipe *Lymnocryptes minimus* | w5 | |
| Snipe *Gallinago gallinago* | s5 p2 w2 | |
| Great Snipe *Gallinago media* | A | |
| Long-billed Dowitcher *Limnodromus scolopaceus* | A | * |

| SPECIES | STATUS | ADDITIONAL INFORMATION |
|---|---|---|
| Woodcock *Scolopax rusticola* | w5 | |
| Black-tailed Godwit *Limosa limosa* | w2 p2 | |
| Bar-tailed Godwit *Limosa lapponica* | w3 p2 | |
| Whimbrel *Numenius phaeopus* | w5 p3 | |
| Slender-billed Curlew *Numenius tenuirostris* | A | no recent records |
| Curlew *Numenius arquata* | w3 p3 | |
| Upland Sandpiper *Bartramia longicauda* | A | |
| Spotted Redshank *Tringa erythropus* | w4 p3 | |
| Redshank *Tringa totanus* | w1 p1 | some breeding records |
| Marsh Sandpiper *Tringa stagnatilis* | A | * |
| Greenshank *Tringa nebularia* | w3 p3 | |
| Greater Yellowlegs *Tringa melanoleuca* | A | * |
| Lesser Yellowlegs *Tringa flavipes* | A | * |
| Solitary Sandpiper *Tringa solitaria* | A | * |
| Green Sandpiper *Tringa ochropus* | w3 p3 | |
| Wood Sandpiper *Tringa glareola* | p4 | |
| Spotted Sandpiper *Actitis macularia* | A | * |
| Common Sandpiper *Actitis hypoleucos* | r3 p2 | |
| Turnstone *Arenaria interpres* | w3 p2 | |
| Wilson's Phalarope *Phalaropus tricolor* | A | * |
| Red-necked Phalarope *Phalaropus lobatus* | p5 | |
| Grey Phalarope *Phalaropus fulicarius* | p5 | * |
| Pomarine Skua *Stercorarius pomarinus* | w4 p4 | |
| Arctic Skua *Stercorarius parasiticus* | w3 p3 | |
| Long-tailed Skua *Stercorarius longicaudus* | A | *regular offshore |
| Great Skua *Catharacta skua* | w3 p3 | |
| Mediterranean Gull *Larus melanocephalus* | w3 p2 | |
| Laughing Gull *Larus atricilla* | A | * |
| Little Gull *Larus minutus* | p4 w5 | |
| Sabine's Gull *Larus sabini* | p5 | *regular offshore |
| Bonaparte's Gull *Larus philadelphia* | A | * |
| Black-headed Gull *Larus ridibundus* | w1 p1 r5 | one breeding record |
| Slender-billed Gull *Larus genei* | A | |
| Audouin's Gull *Larus audouinii* | p5 | *apparently increasing |
| Ring-billed Gull *Larus delawarensis* | w5 | * apparently increasing |
| Common Gull *Larus canus* | w4 | |
| Lesser Black-backed Gull *Larus fuscus* | r5 p1 w1 | a few pairs may breed Berlengas |
| Yellow-legged Gull *Larus cachinnans* | r1 | |
| Herring Gull *Larus argentatus* | w5 | |
| Iceland Gull *Larus glaucoides* | A | * |
| Glaucous Gull *Larus hyperboreus* | A | * |
| Great Black-backed Gull *Larus marinus* | w4 | |
| Black-legged Kittiwake *Rissa tridactyla* | w3 | has bred Berlengas Islands 1980 |
| Gull-billed Tern *Gelochelidon nilotica* | p4 | |
| Caspian Tern *Sterna caspia* | w4 p4 | |
| Royal Tern *Sterna maxima* | A | * |
| Sandwich Tern *Sterna sandvicensis* | w2 p1 | |
| Roseate Tern *Sterna dougallii* | p5 | very few records in the last 10 years |
| Common Tern *Sterna hirundo* | p2 r5 | Bred 1937, 1992, 1993 |

| SPECIES | STATUS | ADDITIONAL INFORMATION |
|---|---|---|
| Arctic Tern *Sterna paradisaea* | p5 | regular in autumn |
| Forster's Tern *Sterna forsteri* | A | * |
| Little Tern *Sterna albifrons* | s3 p2 | |
| Whiskered Tern *Chlidonias hybridus* | s4 p4 | numbers fluctuate markedly |
| Black Tern *Chlidonias niger* | p3 | |
| White-winged Black Tern *Chlidonias leucopterus* | p5 | * scarce and irregular, both seasons |
| Common Guillemot *Uria aalge* | r5 | decreasing |
| Razorbill *Alca torda* | w2 | |
| Little Auk *Alle alle* | A | * |
| Atlantic Puffin *Fratercula arctica* | w5 | |
| Black-bellied Sandgrouse *Pterocles orientalis* | r4 | |
| Pin-tailed Sandgrouse *Pterocles alchata* | r5 | extremely rare |
| Rock Dove *Columba livia* | r3 | purity of species not established |
| Stock Dove *Columba oenas* | w4 p4 s5 | |
| Woodpigeon *Columba palumbus* | r3 w1 | |
| Collared Dove *Streptopelia decaocto* | r3 | breeding range is still expanding |
| Turtle Dove *Streptopelia turtur* | s3 p2 | |
| Oriental Turtle Dove *Streptopelia orientalis* | A | no recent records |
| Great Spotted Cuckoo *Clamator glandarius* | s4 p4 | occurs February to August only |
| Cuckoo *Cuculus canorus* | s2 p4 | |
| Barn Owl *Tyto alba* | r3 | |
| Scops Owl *Otus scops* | s3 p4 | most common in Northeast |
| Eagle Owl *Bubo bubo* | r4 | |
| Little Owl *Athene noctua* | r2 | |
| Tawny Owl *Strix aluco* | r2 | |
| Long-eared Owl *Asio otus* | r4 w4 | |
| Short-eared Owl *Asio flammeus* | w5 | very scarce |
| Marsh Owl *Asio capensis* | A | last recorded 19th century |
| European Nightjar *Caprimulgus europaeus* | s3 p4 | more common in the North |
| Red-necked Nightjar *Caprimulgus ruficollis* | s3 p4 | more common in the South |
| Swift *Apus apus* | s1 p1 | |
| Pallid Swift *Apus pallidus* | s2 p2 | more common in the South |
| Alpine Swift *Apus melba* | s3 p3 | |
| White-rumped Swift *Apus caffer* | s5 | * |
| Little Swift *Apus affinis* | A | * |
| Kingfisher *Alcedo atthis* | r3 p3 | |
| Bee-eater *Merops apiaster* | s2 p2 | |
| Roller *Coracias garrulus* | s4 p4 | |
| Hoopoe *Upupa epops* | r2 p2 | resident in southern half only |
| Wryneck *Jynx torquilla* | s4 p4 w5 | more common in NE, winters S |
| Green Woodpecker *Picus viridis* | r3 | |
| Black Woodpecker *Dryocopus martius* | A | |
| Great Spotted Woodpecker *Dendrocopos major* | r3 | |
| Middle Spotted Woodpecker *Dendrocopos medius* | A | |
| Lesser Spotted Woodpecker *Dendrocopos minor* | r4 | |

| SPECIES | STATUS | ADDITIONAL INFORMATION |
|---|---|---|
| Dupont's Lark *Chersophilus duponti* | A | |
| Calandra Lark *Melanocorypha calandra* | r4 | |
| Short-toed Lark *Calandrella brachydactyla* | s2 p3 | |
| Lesser Short-toed Lark *Calandrella rufescens* | r5 | apparently only at Castro Marim |
| Crested Lark *Galerida cristata* | r2 | |
| Thekla Lark *Galerida theklae* | r2 | |
| Woodlark *Lullula arborea* | r2 | |
| Skylark *Alauda arvensis* | r3 w1 | |
| Sand Martin *Riparia riparia* | s2 p2 | |
| Crag Martin *Ptyonoprogne rupestris* | r3 w3 | |
| Barn Swallow *Hirundo rustica* | s1 p1 w5 | |
| Red-rumped Swallow *Hirundo daurica* | s3 p3 | more common in inner Alentejo |
| House Martin *Delichon urbica* | s1 p1 | occasionally recorded in winter |
| Richard's Pipit *Anthus richardi* | A | *possibly regular wintering |
| Tawny Pipit *Anthus campestris* | s3 p3 w5 | |
| Olive-backed Pipit *Anthus hodgsoni* | A | * |
| Tree Pipit *Anthus trivialis* | s5 p2 | breeds only in the North |
| Meadow Pipit *Anthus pratensis* | w1 | |
| Red-throated Pipit *Anthus cervinus* | p5 | |
| Rock Pipit *Anthus petrosus* | w5 | * |
| Water Pipit *Anthus spinoletta* | s5 w3 | |
| Citrine Wagtail *Motacilla citreola* | A | * |
| Yellow Wagtail *Motacilla flava* | s2 p2 | |
| Grey Wagtail *Motacilla cinerea* | r3 w3 | |
| Pied Wagtail *Motacilla alba* | r2 w1 | race *yarrellii* regular in winter |
| Waxwing *Bombycilla garrulus* | A | |
| Dipper *Cinclus cinclus* | r4 | |
| Wren *Troglodytes troglodytes* | r2 | |
| Hedge Accentor *Prunella modularis* | r3 w2 | |
| Alpine Accentor *Prunella collaris* | w5 | rare and very localised |
| Rufous Bushchat *Cercotrichas galactotes* | s4 p5 | breeds mainly in southeast |
| European Robin *Erithacus rubecula* | r2 p1 w1 | |
| Nightingale *Luscinia megarhynchos* | s2 p2 | |
| Bluethroat *Luscinia svecica* | w3 p2 | bred 1993 at Serra da Estrela |
| Black Redstart *Phoenicurus ochruros* | r3 p3 w2 | |
| Redstart *Phoenicurus phoenicurus* | s4 p3 | |
| Whinchat *Saxicola rubetra* | s5 p3 | breeds northern mountains only |
| Stonechat *Saxicola torquata* | r1 | Siberian race accidental (*) |
| Wheatear *Oenanthe oenanthe* | s3 p2 | |
| Black-eared Wheatear *Oenanthe hispanica* | s3 p3 | |
| Black Wheatear *Oenanthe leucura* | r5 | very localised |
| Rock Thrush *Monticola saxatilis* | s4 p5 | |
| Blue Rock Thrush *Monticola solitarius* | r3 | |
| Ring Ouzel *Turdus torquatus* | w5 p5 | |
| Blackbird *Turdus merula* | r1 | |
| Eyebrowed Thrush *Turdus obscurus* | A | * |
| Fieldfare *Turdus pilaris* | w4 | |
| Song Thrush *Turdus philomelos* | s5 w1 | extremely rare breeder in North |
| Redwing *Turdus iliacus* | w2 | |

| SPECIES | STATUS | ADDITIONAL INFORMATION |
|---|---|---|
| Mistle Thrush *Turdus viscivorus* | r3 | |
| Cetti's Warbler *Cettia cetti* | r2 | |
| Fan-tailed Warbler *Cisticola juncidis* | r1 | |
| Grasshopper Warbler *Locustella naevia* | p3 | |
| Savi's Warbler *Locustella luscinioides* | s4 | very localised |
| Moustached Warbler *Acrocephalus melanopogon* | A | |
| Aquatic Warbler *Acrocephalus paludicola* | p5 | very scarce |
| Sedge Warbler *Acrocephalus schoenobaenus* | p4 | |
| Paddyfield Warbler *Acrocephalus agricola* | A | * |
| Marsh Warbler *Acrocephalus palustris* | A | |
| Reed Warbler *Acrocephalus scirpaceus* | s2 p2 | |
| Great Reed Warbler *Acrocephalus arundinaceus* | s2 | |
| Olivaceous Warbler *Hippolais pallida* | s5 | very scarce |
| Icterine Warbler *Hippolais icterina* | A | |
| Melodious Warbler *Hippolais polyglotta* | s2 p2 | |
| Dartford Warbler *Sylvia undata* | r3 | |
| Spectacled Warbler *Sylvia conspicillata* | s4 p4 | |
| Subalpine Warbler *Sylvia cantillans* | s3 p3 | more common in Northeast |
| Ménétries's Warbler *Sylvia mystacea* | A | |
| Sardinian Warbler *Sylvia melanocephala* | r1 | |
| Orphean Warbler *Sylvia hortensis* | s4 p5 | |
| Lesser Whitethroat *Sylvia curruca* | A | |
| Whitethroat *Sylvia communis* | s4 p3 | |
| Garden Warbler *Sylvia borin* | s5 p1 | scarce breeder in the North |
| Blackcap *Sylvia atricapilla* | r2 w1 | |
| Pallas's Leaf Warbler *Phylloscopus proregulus* | A | * |
| Yellow-browed Warbler *Phylloscopus inornatus* | A | *autumn records almost annual |
| Dusky Warbler *Phylloscopus fuscatus* | A | * |
| Bonelli's Warbler *Phylloscopus bonelli* | s3 p3 | |
| Wood Warbler *Phylloscopus sibilatrix* | A | |
| Chiffchaff *Phylloscopus collybita* | s5 p1 w1 | |
| Iberian Chiffchaff *Phylloscopus brehmii* | s2 p3 | |
| Willow Warbler *Phylloscopus trochilus* | p1 | |
| Goldcrest *Regulus regulus* | w5 | |
| Firecrest *Regulus ignicapillus* | r3 w3 | |
| Spotted Flycatcher *Muscicapa striata* | s4 p2 | |
| Red-breasted Flycatcher *Ficedula parva* | A | * |
| Collared Flycatcher *Ficedula albicollis* | A | |
| Pied Flycatcher *Ficedula hypoleuca* | p1 | |
| Long-tailed Tit *Aegithalos caudatus* | r3 | |
| Marsh Tit *Parus palustris* | A | one ringing recovery from (Belgium) |
| Crested Tit *Parus cristatus* | r3 | |
| Coal Tit *Parus ater* | r3 | |
| Blue Tit *Parus caeruleus* | r1 | |
| Great Tit *Parus major* | r1 | |
| Nuthatch *Sitta europaea* | r3 | |
| Wallcreeper *Tichodroma muraria* | A | |
| Short-toed Treecreeper *Certhia brachydactyla* | r2 | |
| Penduline Tit *Remiz pendulinus* | s5 w3 | very local breeder |

| SPECIES | STATUS | ADDITIONAL INFORMATION |
|---|---|---|
| Golden Oriole *Oriolus oriolus* | s2 p3 | |
| Red-backed Shrike *Lanius collurio* | s4 p5 | breeds in the extreme north |
| Lesser Grey Shrike *Lanius minor* | A | |
| Southern Grey Shrike *Lanius meridionalis* | r2 | |
| Woodchat Shrike *Lanius senator* | s2 p2 | |
| Jay *Garrulus glandarius* | r2 | |
| Azure-winged Magpie *Cyanopica cyana* | r2 | |
| Black-billed Magpie *Pica pica* | r2 | |
| Nutcracker *Nucifraga caryocatactes* | A | |
| Alpine Chough *Pyrrhocorax graculus* | A | |
| Red-billed Chough *Pyrrhocorax pyrrhocorax* | r4 | very localised |
| Jackdaw *Corvus monedula* | r3 | |
| Rook *Corvus frugilegus* | A | |
| Carrion Crow *Corvus corone* | r2 | |
| Raven *Corvus corax* | r3 | |
| Starling *Sturnus vulgaris* | w2 | |
| Spotless Starling *Sturnus unicolor* | r1 | |
| Rosy Starling *Sturnus roseus* | A | * |
| House Sparrow *Passer domesticus* | r1 | |
| Spanish Sparrow *Passer hispaniolensis* | s3 w4 | possibly expanding its range |
| Tree Sparrow *Passer montanus* | r2 p4 | |
| Rock Sparrow *Petronia petronia* | r3 | |
| Snowfinch *Montifringilla nivalis* | A | |
| Chaffinch *Fringilla coelebs* | r1 w1 | |
| Brambling *Fringilla montifringilla* | w4 | |
| Serin *Serinus serinus* | r1 | |
| Citril Finch *Serinus citrinella* | A | |
| Greenfinch *Carduelis chloris* | r1 | |
| Goldfinch *Carduelis carduelis* | r1 w1 | |
| Siskin *Carduelis spinus* | w3 | |
| Linnet *Carduelis cannabina* | r1 | |
| Twite *Carduelis flavirostris* | A | |
| Redpoll *Carduelis flammea* | A | * |
| Crossbill *Loxia curvirostra* | r5 p4 w5 | numbers fluctuate markedly |
| Common Rosefinch *Carpodacus erythrinus* | A | * |
| Trumpeter Finch *Bucanetes githagineus* | A | * |
| Bullfinch *Pyrrhula pyrrhula* | r4 w4 | |
| Hawfinch *Coccothraustes coccothraustes* | r3 | |
| Lapland Bunting *Calcarius lapponicus* | A | * |
| Snow Bunting *Plectrophenax nivalis* | w5 p5 | |
| Yellowhammer *Emberiza citrinella* | r5 | |
| Cirl Bunting *Emberiza cirlus* | r2 | |
| Rock Bunting *Emberiza cia* | r2 | common in North, scarce in South |
| Ortolan Bunting *Emberiza hortulana* | s4 p3 | scarce on spring passage |
| Rustic Bunting *Emberiza rustica* | A | * |
| Little Bunting *Emberiza pusilla* | A | * |
| Yellow-breasted Bunting *Emberiza aureola* | A | * |
| Reed Bunting *Emberiza schoeniclus* | r4 w3 | |
| Corn Bunting *Miliaria calandra* | r1 | in winter flocks may number 100's |

**Introduced Birds**

| | |
|---|---|
| Marabou Stork *Leptopilos crumeniferus* | A |
| Black Francolin *Francolinus francolinus* | r5 |
| Pheasant *Phasianus colchicus* | r4 |
| Rose-ringed Parakeet *Psittacula krameri* | r5 |
| Village Weaver *Ploceus cucullatus* | r5 |
| Yellow-crowned Bishop *Euplectes afer* | r5 |
| Red Bishop *Euplectes orix* | r5 |
| Black-rumped Waxbill *Estrilda troglodytes* | r5 |
| Common Waxbill *Estrilda astrild* | r2 |
| Red Avadavat *Amandava amandava* | r5 |
| Zebra Finch *Taeniopygia guttata* | r5 |
| African Silverbill *Lonchura cantans* | r5 |
| Black-headed Munia *Lonchura malacca* | r5 |
| White-headed Munia *Lonchura maja* | r5 |
| Cut-throat *Amadina fasciata* | r5 |

# Madeira and Selvagens Full Species List

The list contains all known records of birds from the archipelagos of Madeira, Desertas and Selvagens. Old, undocumented records are being verified by the Portuguese Rarities Committee. The meaning of symbols used is the same as for mainland Portugal.

| SPECIES | STATUS | ADDITIONAL INFORMATION |
|---|---|---|
| Great Northern Diver *Gavia immer* | A | |
| Little Grebe *Tachybaptus ruficollis* | A | |
| Slavonian Grebe *Podiceps auritus* | A | |
| Black-necked Grebe *Podiceps nigricollis* | A | |
| Zino's Petrel *Pterodroma madeira* | r5 | |
| Fea's Petrel *Pterodroma feae* | r5 | |
| Bulwer's Petrel *Bulweria bulwerii* | s3 | |
| Cory's Shearwater *Calonectris diomedea* | r2 | |
| Great Shearwater *Puffinus gravis* | p5 | |
| Manx Shearwater *Puffinus puffinus* | s4 | |
| Balearic Shearwater *Puffinus mauretanicus* | A | |
| Little Shearwater *Puffinus assimilis* | r4 | |
| Wilson's Storm Petrel *Oceanites oceanicus* | A | |
| White-faced Storm Petrel *Pelagodroma marina* | s3 | breeds in winter |
| European Storm Petrel *Hydrobates pelagicus* | A | probably overlooked |
| Leach's Storm Petrel *Oceanodroma leucorhoa* | A | probably overlooked |
| Swinhoe's Storm Petrel *Oceanodroma monorhis* | A | may have bred in Selvagens |
| Madeiran Storm Petrel *Oceanodroma castro* | r3 s3 | |
| Red-billed Tropicbird *Phaethon aethereus* | A | |
| Gannet *Morus bassanus* | A | |
| Cormorant *Phalacrocorax carbo* | A | |
| Shag *Phalacrocorax aristotelis* | A | |
| Bittern *Botaurus stellaris* | A | |
| Little Bittern *Ixobrychus minutus* | A | |

| SPECIES | STATUS | ADDITIONAL INFORMATION |
|---|---|---|
| Black-crowned Night Heron | | |
|    *Nycticorax nycticorax* | A | |
| Squacco Heron *Ardeola ralloides* | A | |
| Cattle Egret *Bubulcus ibis* | p5 | |
| Western Reef Egret *Egretta gularis* | A | |
| Little Egret *Egretta garzetta* | r4 | |
| Grey Heron *Ardea cinerea* | r4 | |
| Purple Heron *Ardea purpurea* | p5 | |
| Black Stork *Ciconia nigra* | A | |
| White Stork *Ciconia ciconia* | A | |
| Glossy Ibis *Plegadis falcinellus* | A | |
| Spoonbill *Platalea leucorodia* | A | |
| Bean Goose *Anser fabalis* | A | |
| Pink-footed Goose *Anser brachyrhynchus* | A | |
| White-fronted Goose *Anser albifrons* | A | |
| Greylag Goose *Anser anser* | A | |
| Ruddy Shelduck *Tadorna ferruginea* | A | |
| Shelduck *Tadorna tadorna* | A | |
| Wigeon *Anas penelope* | A | |
| Teal *Anas crecca* | p5 | |
| Mallard *Anas platyrhynchos* | p5 | |
| Pintail *Anas acuta* | A | |
| Shoveler *Anas clypeata* | A | |
| Marbled Duck *Marmaronetta angustirostris* | A | |
| Pochard *Aythya ferina* | A | |
| Ring-necked Duck *Aythya collaris* | A | |
| Tufted Duck *Aythya fuligula* | A | |
| Scaup *Aythya marila* | A | |
| Long-tailed Duck *Clangula hyemalis* | A | |
| Black Scoter *Melanitta nigra* | A | |
| Surf Scoter *Melanitta perspicillata* | A | |
| Goldeneye *Bucephala clangula* | A | |
| Red-breasted Merganser *Mergus serrator* | A | |
| Honey-buzzard *Pernis apivorus* | A | |
| Black Kite *Milvus migrans* | p5 | |
| Red Kite *Milvus milvus* | A | |
| Egyptian Vulture *Neophron percnopterus* | A | |
| Marsh Harrier *Circus aeruginosus* | A | |
| Montagu's Harrier *Circus pygargus* | A | |
| Sparrowhawk *Accipiter nisus* | r5 | |
| Buzzard *Buteo buteo* | r4 | |
| Long-legged Buzzard *Buteo rufinus* | A | |
| Osprey *Pandion haliaetus* | A | |
| Lesser Kestrel *Falco naumanni* | A | |
| Kestrel *Falco tinnunculus* | r3 | |
| Merlin *Falco columbarius* | A | |
| Hobby *Falco subbuteo* | A | |
| Eleonora's Falcon *Falco eleonorae* | A | |
| Peregrine Falcon *Falco peregrinus* | A | |

| SPECIES | STATUS | ADDITIONAL INFORMATION |
|---|---|---|
| Barbary Falcon *Falco pelegrinoides* | A | |
| Red-legged Partridge *Alectoris rufa* | r4 | |
| Quail *Coturnix coturnix* | r5 | |
| Pheasant *Phasianus colchicus* | | introduced |
| Helmeted Guineafowl *Numida meleagris* | | introduced |
| Water Rail *Rallus aquaticus* | A | |
| Spotted Crake *Porzana porzana* | A | |
| Little Crake *Porzana parva* | A | |
| Baillon's Crake *Porzana pusilla* | A | |
| African Black Crake *Limnocorax flavirostra* | A | |
| Corncrake *Crex crex* | A | |
| Moorhen *Gallinula chloropus* | p5 | |
| Allen's Gallinule *Porphyrula alleni* | A | |
| American Purple Gallinule *Porphyrula martinica* | A | |
| Purple Swamp-hen *Porphyrio porphyrio* | A | |
| Coot *Fulica atra* | p5 | |
| Crane *Grus grus* | A | |
| Little Bustard *Tetrax tetrax* | A | |
| Oystercatcher *Haematopus ostralegus* | A | |
| African Black Oystercatcher *Haematopus moquini* | A | |
| Black-winged Stilt *Himantopus himantopus* | A | |
| Avocet *Recurvirostra avosetta* | A | |
| Stone-curlew *Burhinus oedicnemus* | A | |
| Cream-coloured Courser *Cursorius cursor* | A | |
| Collared Pratincole *Glareola pratincola* | A | |
| Little Ringed Plover *Charadrius dubius* | s5 | |
| Great Ringed Plover *Charadrius hiaticula* | p5 | |
| Killdeer *Charadrius vociferus* | A | |
| Kentish Plover *Charadrius alexandrinus* | r5 | |
| Dotterel *Charadrius morinellus* | A | |
| Golden Plover *Pluvialis apricaria* | A | |
| Grey Plover *Pluvialis squatarola* | A | |
| Lapwing *Vanellus vanellus* | w5 p5 | |
| Knot *Calidris canutus* | p5 | |
| Sanderling *Calidris alba* | p5 | |
| Semi-palmated Sandpiper *Calidris pusilla* | A | |
| Little Stint *Calidris minuta* | p5 | |
| Western Sandpiper *Calidris mauri* | A | |
| White-rumped Sandpiper *Calidris fuscicollis* | A | |
| Pectoral Sandpiper *Calidris melanotos* | A | |
| Curlew Sandpiper *Calidris ferruginea* | p5 | |
| Purple Sandpiper *Calidris maritima* | A | |
| Dunlin *Calidris alpina* | p4 | |
| Ruff *Philomachus pugnax* | p5 | |
| Jack Snipe *Lymnocryptes minimus* | p5 | |
| Snipe *Gallinago gallinago* | w4 | |
| Great Snipe *Gallinago media* | A | |

| SPECIES | STATUS | ADDITIONAL INFORMATION |
|---|---|---|
| Woodcock *Scolopax rusticola* | r4 | |
| Black-tailed Godwit *Limosa limosa* | p5 | |
| Bar-tailed Godwit *Limosa lapponica* | p5 | |
| Whimbrel *Numenius phaeopus* | p4 | |
| Curlew *Numenius arquata* | p5 | |
| Upland Sandpiper *Bartramia longicauda* | A | |
| Spotted Redshank *Tringa erythropus* | A | |
| Redshank *Tringa totanus* | p5 | |
| Greenshank *Tringa nebularia* | p5 | |
| Lesser Yellowlegs *Tringa flavipes* | A | |
| Green Sandpiper *Tringa ochropus* | A | |
| Wood Sandpiper *Tringa glareola* | A | |
| Common Sandpiper *Actitis hypoleucos* | p5 | |
| Spotted Sandpiper *Actitis macularia* | A | |
| Turnstone *Arenaria interpres* | p4 w5 | |
| Wilson's Phalarope *Phalaropus tricolor* | A | |
| Red-necked Phalarope *Phalaropus lobatus* | A | |
| Grey Phalarope *Phalaropus fulicarius* | A | |
| Pomarine Skua *Stercorarius pomarinus* | p5 | |
| Arctic Skua *Stercorarius parasiticus* | p5 | |
| Long-tailed Skua *Stercorarius longicaudus* | p5 | |
| Great Skua *Catharacta skua* | p5 | |
| Great Black-headed Gull *Larus ichthyaetus* | A | |
| Mediterranean Gull *Larus melanocephalus* | p5 | |
| Franklin's Gull *Larus pipixcan* | A | |
| Little Gull *Larus minutus* | A | |
| Sabine's Gull *Larus sabini* | A | |
| Black-headed Gull *Larus ridibundus* | p4 w5 | |
| Ring-billed Gull *Larus delawarensis* | w5 | |
| Common Gull *Larus canus* | A | |
| Lesser Black-backed Gull *Larus fuscus* | p3 w3 | |
| Herring Gull *Larus argentatus* | A | |
| Yellow-legged Gull *Larus cachinnans* | r2 | |
| Iceland Gull *Larus glaucoides* | A | |
| Glaucous Gull *Larus hyperboreus* | A | |
| Great Black-backed Gull *Larus marinus* | A | |
| Black-legged Kittiwake *Rissa tridactyla* | w5 p5 | |
| Gull-billed Tern *Gelochelidon nilotica* | A | |
| Caspian Tern *Sterna caspia* | A | |
| Sandwich Tern *Sterna sandvicensis* | A | |
| Roseate Tern *Sterna dougallii* | s5 | |
| Common Tern *Sterna hirundo* | s3 | |
| Arctic Tern *Sterna paradisaea* | A | |
| Sooty Tern *Sterna fuscata* | A | probably bred Selvagens |
| Little Tern *Sterna albifrons* | A | |
| Whiskered Tern *Chlidonias hybridus* | A | |
| Black Tern *Chlidonias niger* | A | |
| White-winged Tern *Chlidonias leucopterus* | A | |
| Little Auk *Alle alle* | A | |

| SPECIES | STATUS | ADDITIONAL INFORMATION |
|---|---|---|
| Puffin *Fratercula arctica* | A | |
| Rock Dove *Columba livia* | r3 | |
| Woodpigeon *Columba palumbus* | A | Madeiran race extinct |
| Long-toed Pigeon *Columba trocaz* | r4 | |
| Collared Dove *Streptopelia decaocto* | A | |
| Turtle Dove *Streptopelia turtur* | p5 | |
| Great Spotted Cuckoo *Clamator glandarius* | A | |
| Cuckoo *Cuculus canorus* | A | |
| Barn Owl *Tyto alba* | r4 | |
| Scops Owl *Otus scops* | A | |
| Short-eared Owl *Asio flammeus* | p5 w5 | |
| European Nightjar *Caprimulgus europaeus* | A | |
| Red-necked Nightjar *Caprimulgus ruficollis* | A | |
| Plain Swift *Apus unicolor* | s3 | |
| Swift *Apus apus* | p5 | |
| Pallid Swift *Apus pallidus* | s5 | |
| Alpine Swift *Apus melba* | A | |
| Little Swift *Apus affinis* | A | |
| Kingfisher *Alcedo atthis* | A | |
| Bee-eater *Merops apiaster* | p5 | |
| Roller *Coracias garrulus* | p5 | |
| Hoopoe *Upupa epops* | s5 p5 | |
| Wryneck *Jynx torquilla* | A | |
| Calandra Lark *Melanocorypha calandra* | A | |
| Short-toed Lark *Calandrella brachydactyla* | A | |
| Skylark *Alauda arvensis* | p5 w5 | |
| Sand Martin *Riparia riparia* | p5 | |
| Crag Martin *Ptyonoprogne rupestris* | A | |
| Barn Swallow *Hirundo rustica* | p5 | |
| Red-rumped Swallow *Hirundo daurica* | A | |
| House Martin *Delichon urbica* | p5 | |
| Tawny Pipit *Anthus campestris* | A | |
| Berthelot's Pipit *Anthus berthelotii* | r4 | |
| Tree Pipit *Anthus trivialis* | A | |
| Meadow Pipit *Anthus pratensis* | A | |
| Red-throated Pipit *Anthus cervinus* | A | |
| Yellow Wagtail *Motacilla flava* | p5 | |
| Grey Wagtail *Motacilla cinerea* | r3 | |
| Pied Wagtail *Motacilla alba* | p5 | |
| Wren *Troglodytes troglodytes* | A | |
| Rufous Bushchat *Cercotrichas galactotes* | A | |
| Robin *Erithacus rubecula* | r3 w3 | |
| Nightingale *Luscinia megarhynchos* | p5 | |
| Black Redstart *Phoenicurus ochruros* | p5 | |
| Redstart *Phoenicurus phoenicurus* | p5 | |
| Whinchat *Saxicola rubetra* | p5 | |
| Stonechat *Saxicola torquata* | A | |
| Isabelline Wheater *Oenanthe isabellina* | A | |
| Wheatear *Oenanthe oenanthe* | p5 | |

| SPECIES | STATUS | ADDITIONAL INFORMATION |
|---|---|---|
| Desert Wheatear *Oenanthe deserti* | A | |
| Rock Thrush *Monticola saxatilis* | A | |
| Ring Ouzel *Turdus torquatus* | A | |
| Blackbird *Turdus merula* | r3 | |
| Red-throated Thrush *Turdus ruficollis* | A | |
| Fieldfare *Turdus pilaris* | A | |
| Song Thrush *Turdus philomelos* | A | |
| Redwing *Turdus iliacus* | w5 | |
| Mistle Thrush *Turdus viscivorus* | w5 | |
| Fan-tailed Warbler *Cisticola juncidis* | A | |
| Grasshopper Warbler *Locustella naevia* | p5 | |
| River Warbler *Locustella fluviatilis* | A | |
| Sedge Warbler *Acrocephalus schoenobaenus* | p5 | |
| Marsh Warbler *Acrocephalus palustris* | A | |
| Reed Warbler *Acrocephalus scirpaceus* | p5 | |
| Great Reed Warbler *Acrocephalus arundinaceus* | A | |
| Olivaceous Warbler *Hippolais pallida* | A | |
| Icterine Warbler *Hippolais icterina* | A | |
| Melodious Warbler *Hippolais polyglotta* | p5 | |
| Spectacled Warbler *Sylvia conspicillata* | r5 | |
| Subalpine Warbler *Sylvia cantillans* | A | |
| Orphean Warbler *Sylvia hortensis* | A | |
| Sardinian Warbler *Sylvia melanocephala* | A | |
| Lesser Whitethroat *Sylvia curruca* | A | |
| Whitethroat *Sylvia communis* | p5 | |
| Garden Warbler *Sylvia borin* | p5 | |
| Blackcap *Sylvia atricapilla* | r2 | |
| Yellow-browed Warbler *Phylloscopus inornatus* | A | |
| Bonelli's Warbler *Phylloscopus bonelli* | A | |
| Wood Warbler *Phylloscopus sibilatrix* | A | |
| Chiffchaff *Phylloscopus collybita* | w5 p5 | |
| Willow Warbler *Phylloscopus trochilus* | p5 | |
| Firecrest *Regulus ignicapillus* | r4 | |
| Spotted Flycatcher *Muscicapa striata* | p5 | |
| Red-breasted Flycatcher *Ficedula parva* | A | |
| Pied Flycatcher *Ficedula hypoleuca* | p5 | |
| Golden Oriole *Oriolus oriolus* | p5 | |
| Red-backed Shrike *Lanius collurio* | A | |
| Woodchat Shrike *Lanius senator* | p5 | |
| Jackdaw *Corvus monedula* | A | |
| Rook *Corvus frugilegus* | A | |
| Starling *Sturnus vulgaris* | w5 | |
| Spotless Starling *Sturnus unicolor* | A | |
| Rosy Starling *Sturnus roseus* | A | |
| Spanish Sparrow *Passer hispaniolensis* | r5 | |
| Rock Sparrow *Petronia petronia* | r4 | |
| Chaffinch *Fringilla coelebs* | r3 | |
| Brambling *Fringilla montifringilla* | A | |
| Serin *Serinus serinus* | A | |

| SPECIES | STATUS | ADDITIONAL INFORMATION |
|---|---|---|
| Canary *Serinus canaria* | r3 | |
| Greenfinch *Carduelis chloris* | A | |
| Goldfinch *Carduelis carduelis* | r3 | |
| Siskin *Carduelis spinus* | A | |
| Linnet *Carduelis cannabina* | r5 | |
| Crossbill *Loxia curvirostra* | A | |
| Hawfinch *Coccothraustes coccothraustes* | A | |
| Yellow Warbler *Dendroica petechia* | A | |
| American Redstart *Setophaga ruticilla* | A | |
| Snow Bunting *Plectrophenax nivalis* | A | |
| Ortolan Bunting *Emberiza hortulana* | A | |

# Amphibians and Reptiles (mainland Portugal)

Golden-striped Salamander *Chioglossa lusitanica*
Sharp-ribbed Salamander *Pleurodeles waltl*
Fire Salamander *Salamandra salamandra*
Bosca's Newt *Triturus boscai*
Palmate Newt *Triturus helveticus*
Marbled Newt *Triturus marmoratus*
Iberian Midwife Toad *Alytes cisternasii*
Midwife Toad *Alytes obstetricans*
Painted Frog *Discoglossus galganoi*
Western Spadefoot *Pelobates cultripes*
Parsley Frog *Pelodytes punctatus*
Common Toad *Bufo bufo*
Natterjack *Bufo calamita*
Common Tree Frog *Hyla arborea*
Stripeless Tree Frog *Hyla meridionalis*
Iberian Frog *Rana iberica*
Marsh Frog *Rana perezi*
European Pond Terrapin *Emys orbicularis*
Stripe-necked Terrapin *Mauremys leprosa*
Loggerhead Turtle *Caretta caretta*
Green Sea Turtle *Chelonia midas*
Hawksbill Sea Turtle *Eretmochelys imbricata*
Leathery Turtle *Dermochelys coriacea*
Turkish Gecko *Hemydactylus turcicus*
Moorish Gecko *Tarentola mauritanica*
Mediterranean Chameleon *Chamaeleo chamaeleon*
Slow Worm *Anguis fragilis*
Amphisbaenian *Blanus cinereus*
Spiny-footed Lizard *Acanthodactylus erythrurus*
Ocellated Lizard *Lacerta lepida*
Iberian Rock Lizard *Lacerta monticola*
Schreiber's Green Lizard *Lacerta schreiberi*
Bocage's Wall Lizard *Podarcis bocagei*
Iberian Wall Lizard *Podarcis hispanica*
Large Psammodromus *Psammodromus algirus*

SPECIES
Spanish Psammodromus *Psammodromus hispanicus*
Bedriaga's Skink *Chalcides bedriagai*
Three-toed Skink *Chalcides chalcides*
Horseshoe Snake *Coluber hippocrepis*
Smooth Snake *Coronella austriaca*
Southern Smooth Snake *Coronella girondica*
Ladder Snake *Elaphe scalaris*
False Smooth Snake *Macroprotodon cucculatus*
Montpellier Snake *Malpolon monspessulanus*
Viperine Snake *Natrix maura*
Grass Snake *Natrix natrix*
Lataste's Viper *Vipera latastei*
Iberian Adder *Vipera seoanei*

# Mammals (mainland Portugal)

Western Hedgehog *Erinaceus europaeus*
Pygmy Shrew *Sorex minutus*
Spanish Shrew *Sorex granarius*
Miller's Water Shrew *Neomys anomalus*
Greater Water Shrew *Crocidura russula*
Lesser Water Shrew *Crocidura suaveolens*
Pigmy White-thoothed Shrew *Suncus etruscus*
Pyrenean Desman *Galemys pyrenaicus*
Blind Mole *Talpa occidentalis*
Greater Horseshoe Bat *Rhinolophus ferrumequinum*
Lesser Horseshoe Bat *Rhinolophus hipposideros*
Mediterranean Horseshoe Bat *Rhinolophus euryale*
Mehely's Horseshoe Bat *Rhinolophus mehelyi*
Whiskered Bat *Myotis mystacinus*
Geoffroy's Bat *Myotis emarginatus*
Natterer's Bat *Myotis nattereri*
Bechstein's Bat *Myotis bechsteinii*
Greater Mouse-eared Bat *Myotis myotis*
Lesser Mouse-eared Bat *Myotis blythii*
Daubenton's Bat *Myotis daubentonii*
Common Pipistrelle *Pipistrellus pipistrellus*
Nathusius's Pipistrelle *Pipistrellus nathusii*
Kuhl's Pipistrelle *Pipistrellus kuhli*
Savi's Pipistrelle *Hypsugo savii*
Leisler's Bat *Nyctalus leisleri*
Noctule *Nyctalus noctula*
Greater Noctule *Nyctalus lasiopterus*
Serotine *Eptesicus serotinus*
Barbastelle *Barbastella barbastellus*
Brown Long-eared Bat *Plecotus auritus*
Grey Long-eared Bat *Plecotus austriacus*
Schreiber's Bat *Miniopterus schreibersii*
Free-tailed Bat *Tadarida teniotis*

SPECIES
Brown Hare *Lepus capensis*
Rabbit *Oryctolagus cuniculus*
Squirrel *Sciurus vulgaris*
Northern Water Vole *Arvicola terrestris*
Southwestern Water Vole *Arvicola sapidus*
Cabrera's Vole *Microtus cabrerae*
Field Vole *Microtus agrestis*
Lusitanian Pine Vole *Microtus lusitanicus*
Mediterranean Pine Vole *Microtus duodecimcostatus*
Wood Mouse *Apodemus sylvaticus*
Black Rat *Rattus rattus*
Brown Rat *Rattus norvegicus*
House Mouse *Mus musculus*
Algerian Mouse *Mus spretus*
Garden Dormouse *Eliomys quercinus*
Wolf *Canis lupus*
Red Fox *Vulpes vulpes*
Stoat *Mustela erminea*
Weasel *Mustela nivalis*
American Mink *Mustela vison* intr.
Ferret *Mustela putorius*
Pine Marten *Martes martes*
Beech Marten *Martes foina*
Badger *Meles meles*
Otter *Lutra lutra*
Genet *Genetta genetta*
Egyptian Mongoose *Hespestes ichneumon*
Wild Cat *Felis silvestris*
Iberian Lynx *Lynx pardina*
Grey Seal *Halichoerus grypus*
Common Seal *Phoca vitulina*
Ringed Seal *Phoca hispida*
Hooded Seal *Cystophora cristata*
Bearded Seal *Erignathus barbatus*
Wild Boar *Sus scrofa*
Fallow Deer *Cervus dama*
Red Deer *Cervus elaphus*
Roe Deer *Capreolus capreolus*
Harbour Porpoise *Phocoena phocoena*
Common Dolphin *Delphinus delphis*
Bottlenose Dolphin *Tursiops truncatus*
Striped Dolphin *Stenella coeruleoalba*
False Killer Whale *Pseudorca crassidens*
Killer Whale *Orcinus orca*
Risso's Dolphin *Grampus griseus*
Long-finned Pilot Whale *Globicephala melaena*
Cuvier's Beaked Whale *Ziphius cavirostris*
Blainville's Beaked Whale *Mesoplodon densirostris*
Gervais' Beaked Whale *Mesoplodon europaeus*

Pygmy Sperm Whale *Kogia breviceps*
Sperm Whale *Physeter macrocephalus*
Black Right Whale *Eubalaena glacialis*
Humpback *Megaptera novaeangliae*
Blue Whale *Balaenoptera musculus*
Fin Whale *Balaenoptera physalus*
Sei Whale *Balaenoptera borealis*
Minke Whale *Balaenoptera acutorostrata*

# LOCAL CONTACTS AND SOCIETIES

## Non-governmental organisations

There are several environmental groups in Portugal which undertake conservation projects, some of them concern birds. Quercus and LPN are the most active countrywide and bird-related projects are currently underway. SPEA is the only scientific society so far dealing exclusively with birds; it congregates most Portuguese ornithologists, both professionals and amateurs, and undertakes research and educational activities in this area. The Portuguese Rarities Committee, founded in January 1995, operates as part of SPEA and all sightings of rare birds should be sent to the Committee, via SPEA (a list of species needing homologation can be asked for – see the full species list for further details).

SPEA-Sociedade Portuguesa para o Estudo das Aves
Rua da Vitória, 53-2° Dt°.
1100 Lisboa
tel./fax: 01-3431847

SPEA regularly publishes 'Pardela', an ornithological journal and from 1995 onwards the Portuguese Rarities Committee annual report is to be found there.

QUERCUS – Associação Nacional de Conservação da Natureza
Rua do Salitre, 139, sala 3-A
1100 LISBOA
tel.: 01-3152039

LPN-Liga para a Protecção da Natureza
Estrada do Calhariz de Benfica, 187
1500 LISBOA
Tel. 01-7780097

A ROCHA – A Christian Field Study Centre and Bird Observatory
Cruzinha
8500 MEXILHOEIRA GRANDE
Tel. 082-96380
Fax. 082-969860

## State Bodies

The ICN – Institute for Nature Conservation co-ordinates conservation-related activities in Portugal and all protected areas are coordinated by this body.

CEMPA – 'Centro de Estudos de Migrações e Protecção de Aves' (Bird Protection and Migration Study Centre) is the department of ICN concerned with bird studies and censuses.

ICN – Instituto da Conservação da Natureza
Rua da Lapa, 73
1200 Lisboa
tel.: 01-3950464/5/6
fax: 01-601048

CEMPA
Rua Filipe Folque, 46-5°
1050 Lisboa
tel.: 01-3523018
fax: 01-3574771

A journal called AIRO, published once or twice a year by
ICN/CEMPA, is currently one of the few journals dealing specifically
with birds. It annually published the Iberian Rarities Committee's
report from 1988 to 1994. In 1995, this Committee ceased to exist and a
fully autonomous Portuguese rarities Committee now publishes an
annual report in Pardela (see above).

## Protected areas

In Portugal there are several classes of protected areas: National and
Natural Parks, Nature Reserves and Landscape Protection Areas.

Parque Nacional da Peneda-Gerês
Quinta das Parretas
Rodovia
4700 Braga
tel.: 053-613166/7/8
fax: 053-613169

Parque Natural da Arrábida
Praça da República
2900 Setúbal
tel.: 065-524032
fax: 065-37256

Parque Natural de Montesinho
Bairro Coronel Salvador Nunes Teixeira, Lote 5
Apartado 90
5300 Bragança
tel.: 073-381444
fax: 073-381179

Parque Natural da Ria Formosa
Quinta do Marim
Quelfes
8700 Olhão
tel.: 089-704134/5
fax: 089-704165

Parque Natural da Serra da Estrela
Rua 1° de Maio, 2
Valazedo
6260 Manteigas
tel.: 075-982382/3
fax: 075-982384

Parque Natural da Serra de São Mamede
Praceta Heróis da Índia, 8, 1°
Apartado 162
7301 Portalegre Codex
tel.: 045-27215
fax: 045-27501

Parque Natural das Serras de Aire e Candeeiros
Jardim Municipal
2040 Rio Maior
tel.: 043-91968; 043-90168
fax: 043-92605

Parque Natural de Sintra-Cascais
Rua General Alves Roçadas, 10-1° F.
2710 Sintra
tel.: 01-9235116
fax: 01-9235141

Reserva Natural da Berlenga
Olho de Boi
2800 Cacilhas
tel.: 01-2763154
fax: 01-2745009

Reserva Natural das Dunas de S. Jacinto
3800 S. Jacinto
tel.: 034-331282 (reception), 034-831063 (HQ)
fax: 034-3331189

Reserva Natural do Estuário do Tejo
Av. Combatentes da Grande Guerra, 1
2890 Alcochete
tel.: 01-2341742
fax: 01-2341654

Reserva Natural do Estuário do Sado
Praça da República
2900 Setúbal
tel.: 065-524032
fax: 065-37256

Reserva Natural do Paul de Arzila
Rua Padre António Vieira, 1-1°
3000 Coimbra
tel.: 039-22151/2
fax: 039-25352

Reserva Natural do Paul do Boquilobo
Quinta do Paul
Brogueira
Apartado 27
2350 Riachos
tel.: 049-820550

Reserva Natural do Sapal de Castro Marim e Vila Real de Santo António
Castelo da Vila
8950 Castro Marim
tel.: 081-531141
fax: 081-531257

Parque Natural do Sudoeste Alentejano e Costa Vicentina
Rua Serpa Pinto, 16 r/c Dt°.
7630 Odemira
tel.: 083-22735
fax: 083-22830

Rua João Dias Mendes, 46-A
8670 Aljezur
tel.: 082-98673

**Birding holidays**
Nature tourism is a recent activity in Portugal. There are several companies in the country dealing with this kind of tourism, but so far there is just one for birdwatching activities,

Lanius – Wildlife Tours
Rua 25 de Abril, 35, R/c Dto.
Paivas – 2840 AMORA
Tel./Fax. 043-23643

# RECOMMENDED READING

- Bannerman, D.A. & W.M. Bannerman 1963. *Birds of the Atlantic Islands*, Vol. I. A History of the Birds of the Canary Islands and the Salvages. Oliver & Boyd, Edinburgh & London.
- Bannerman, D.A. & W.M. Bannerman 1965. *Birds of the Atlantic Islands*, Vol. II. A History of the Birds of Madeira. Oliver & Boyd, Edinburgh & London.
- Bolton, M. 1987. *An Atlas of Wintering Birds in the Western Algarve 1986-87*. A Rocha Occasional Publications no. 1.
- Costa, H., J.C. Farinha, C.C. Moore & R. Neves 1993. Lista Sistemática de Espécies de Aves de Ocorrência Acidental, Rara ou Pouco Comum em Portugal Continental. *Airo* 4 (1): 28-33.
- Crespo, E. & M. Oliveira 1989. *Atlas da Distribuição dos Anfíbios e Répteis de Portugal Continental*. Serviço Nacional de Parques Reservas e Conservação da Natureza. Lisboa.
- Díaz, M., B. Asensio & J.L. Tellería 1996. *Aves Ibéricas*, vol I No Passeriformes. J. M. Reyero Editor. Madrid.
- Farinha, J.C. & A. Trindade 1994. *Contribuição para o Inventário e Caracterização de Zonas Húmidas em Portugal Continental*. Publicação MedWet. Instituto da Conservação da Natureza.
- Grimmett, R.F.A. & T.A. Jones (Comp.) 1989. *Important Bird Areas in Europe*. I.C.B.P. Technical Publication no 9. Cambridge.
- Mougin, J.L., F. Roux, P.A.Zino, C. Jouanin, J-C. Stahl & B. Despin 1987. Les Oiseaux visiteurs des Îles Selvagens. *Bol. Mus. Mun. Funchal*, **39** (183): 5-24.
- Pimenta, M. & M. L. Santarém 1996. *Atlas das Aves do Parque Nacional da Peneda-Gerês*. Instituto da Conservação da Natureza.
- Ribeiro, O. & H. Lautensach 1987. *Geografia de Portugal; I. A Posição Geográfica do Território*. Edições João Sá da Costa. Lisboa.
- Ribeiro, O. 1987. *Portugal, o Mediterrâneo e o Atlântico*. Livraria Sá da Costa Editora. Lisboa (5° ed.).
- Rufino, R. (Coord.) 1989. *Atlas das Aves que Nidificam em Portugal Continental*. Serviço Nacional de Parques Reservas e Conservação da Natureza. Lisboa.
- SNPRCN 1990. *Livro Vermelho dos Vertebrados de Portugal*, vol. I. Serviço Nacional de Parques Reservas e Conservação da Natureza. Lisboa.
- Zino, F., M.J.Biscoito & P.A.Zino 1995. Birds of the Archipelago of Madeira and Selvagens – new records and checklist. *Bol. Mus. Mun. Funchal*, **47** (262): 63-100.